Sunnydale: Memory of an Assistant Principal

Written by

Philip R. Mills

For my wife, Whatshername

Chapter 1

"Okay, just roll your finger," she said, as she gently placed her hand above mine and rocked my index finger side to side. She had small hands and I could see they were perfectly manicured. They were soft and her touch felt so light, it had a calming effect on me.

"Just side to side."

"I'm on it," I said, sending all my mental powers to my fingers.

"Wait, we may have to try it again. Oh no, that worked."

The fingerprinting machine beeped and I could see the red bar at the top of the screen turn to green. My fingerprints were in the system. The black swirly lines that looked like small galaxies were now on their way to parts unknown for scrutiny by parties unknown.

She hit a few more keys and the galaxies were replaced with ordinary text. "I see from your information you worked at the school that made all this possible."

"Necessary," I corrected as gently as she had touched my hand.

"Yeah," she smiled.

She had a wide smile that made her thin angular face seem friendly but my stomach jumped into a knot when she mentioned the school. It wasn't my apprehension at the conversation that was surely coming; it was all the horrible memories that would accompany it. I knew they would flood over my consciousness from one side to the other, sloshing back and forth, evoking emotions then drowning them. I also knew that when the flood subsided only rage would be left. I braced for it.

"You were the Principal there?" she asked still smiling, still processing my fingerprints.

"No, I was the assistant principal. I don't work there anymore."

"Oh," the smile fading as if I had just revealed my dog died.

That fading smile gave me small hope that the conversation I dreaded was going to pass us by, but she was the cheery sort of person who is seldom deterred by reality. I love the idea of cheery people but I can't stand to be around them. I tolerate them because I could never figure out a way to justify actually putting into practice my visceral desire to punch them in the face repeatedly.

It wasn't just her behavior that formed my opinion about her cheery disposition. The sign outside her office confirmed it by saying, "Storage." The state decreed that all prospective educators now had to have federal criminal clearance as well as state criminal clearance and she was given the task of handling it for this governmental entity. Literally at the end of the hall, a dank, windowless storage room was converted for the purpose. Placed there at the mercy of the menacing mold spores and left for dead by the powers that be, she didn't partake of the anger she was entitled to. She remained cheery.

"What school did you work at?" she asked, the smile returning, my hope fading.

"It was a combination junior high, high school grades seven through twelve," I said, scrupulously avoiding the name.

"Oh, Sunnydale," the smile now at full mast.

Actually, the school's name was not Sunnydale. That is the name I automatically translate the real name into in my mind because the real name is too painful to hear. I also do the same to all the names of the people I knew there. It's an insane thing to do but nature loves paradox and I know of no better paradox than the truth, which is, in order to remain sane one must sometimes do insane things.

"Yeah."

"That was awful what happened there. Were you working there when it happened?"

"Ohhhh yeah." I added a small chuckle to go with a small smile to cover my tracks.

"That must have been awful."

Just then a man in business attire appeared in the doorway. I would have guessed he was here for the same reason I was but for two things. One, he was standing too comfortably and two; he had a big bag of potato chips in his left hand.

"Oh, this is my husband, Ted; he's the Assistant Executive Director here."

He was an administrator of classic design. Tall, slightly graying hair, slim with well proportioned features and a freakishly close shave. His movements as well as his speech were measured. I have come to believe there is a factory in the Midwest that manufactures administrators like Ted. This guy was so nondescript; a person with a photographic memory couldn't pick him out of a one man lineup.

"Hello," he said extending his hand.

"Hi, Harris Farmer," I said and shook his hand. Inside I cringed. I hate shaking hands.

"He worked at Sunnydale when they had all those problems two years ago," she said, holding back the cheer slightly.

"Oh," he nodded. "That was a terrible situation."

"Yeah."

"It goes to show you that you can do all the checking in the world and you never know."

"Yeah," I said, and I was going to leave it at that but then the flood started. Perhaps it was the naked fluorescent lights and the physical and temporal distance from Sunnydale that prompted me to say, "I'll let you in on a little secret, the school board knew everything and so did the administrators and so did the local police. I was the only one who didn't know anything."

"Hmmm," he nodded slowly and she smiled less brightly.

Immediately after I made that revelation I did what my time as a school administrator trained me to do, an automatic check of what I had just said for errors, misstatements or anything that could come back at me. In the middle of my check I realized I didn't have to do that anymore. I didn't have to talk like an administrator. I could be honest.

It was a moment of liberation as great as any and it relieved the tightness in my chest a little. I relaxed a bit. I told Mr. Wonderful and Mrs. Happy that I enjoyed talking to them even though I knew he would suspect my every word, especially since they were genuine. I smiled broadly and headed back to my car.

Chapter 2

Sunlight sifted by the low, gray cloud cover, only marginally warmed the early May afternoon. I walked semi-hypnotized. It was a dangerous state of mind and I knew it. My thoughts could drift uncontrolled. Not that they would need to be tamed if my mind was otherwise occupied as, say, with a job.

My occupation presently was walking down a deserted dirt road. Despite the best efforts of the leaden clouds, everything, even the dirt on the road was bright and sparkly from a sheen of water laid down by earlier rain.

Somehow it reminded me of the students when they arrived on the morning of the first day of school. They were bright and shiny and bubbling with energy. Socializing proudly in their new clothes, they smiled and joked with light hearted repartee in giddy anticipation of what this new school year would bring.

I shared in it every time even though I knew the coming school year would be, for me anyway, like most any school year. Yet, my vicarious feelings that first day at Sunnydale would prove to be as correct as they would be painful.

I knew it would be a mistake to let my mind even go near the subject but I did it because I wanted to feel the emotional high of the first day. I wanted to feel something.

I had had many first days before Sunnydale, almost fifteen as a teacher. I figured I'd be safe if I didn't let my thoughts linger too long, if I wasn't too greedy. I was wrong.

Just as I was navigating the edge of a rather large mud puddle my mind seized me and hauled me back, dragged me, to that first day at Sunnydale. It took me to precisely eight minutes after the first class started.

The phone rang.

"Harris Farmer, Assistant Principal to the stars," I said as soon as I got the handset to my head.

"Hey Mr. Farmer, this is Mr. Woods. My class isn't here."

"What do you mean the class isn't there? The *whole* class didn't show up!?"

"Yeah! None of them showed up."

"I'm on it," I replied. I hung up the phone and my mind instantly kicked into high gear.

This was a matter which on its face was unfathomable. I had never seen or heard of an entire class missing.

Was it possible that the entire class cut woodshop, I wondered as I was heading out of the office. The principal had told me the students at Sunnydale were like no others in that they were willing and able to stoop to a level of evil none dared go.

My whole nervous system was jazzed by the time I hit the main hallway. This was real bad. The law of students is that if you leave them unattended, they will do something you don't want them to do. And whatever form their misbehavior took it would result in physical injury and or damaged property.

This was eight minutes into the first day and I knew that if any one of the million scenarios playing out in my head came true, I would be the one held accountable. The Principal and the Superintendent would brand me an idiot and that would end my career as an administrator.

I started down to the gym area. Perhaps they're in the gym, I told myself hopefully. Maybe they misread their schedules and went to the gym instead of woodshop. The seventh graders only attended shop class three out of the six days of the six day cycle. The other days of the cycle they had gym or study hall.

I judged the odds of the students all cutting class at the same time unlikely as I headed down the empty corridor. If the students were not in the gym, and they *had* decided to cut class en masse, the likely hiding places were near the gym. The gym was the logical place to start. A little calm began to creep into my mind now that I had logic on my side.

I slowed my walk and tried to look casual as I checked my tracks. No one was paying attention. That is, no one was directly watching me. I knew that the noise from my heels was doing a Doppler effect for every open classroom door I passed. Nearly all eyes would be on me as I passed but that would only provide a quick view of me and not much to hang any suppositions on, although a few probably still would.

Now I was in a rhythm. One loud heart beat, one swish then one heel hitting the floor. It was thud-swish-bang, thud-swish-bang, thud-swish-bang, all the way to the gym. Like most rhythms there was something engaging in it and thus helped to calm my jumping nerves. I almost didn't want to stop walking when I got to the gym doors.

I stopped at the first door in the series of six to check out the gym. It was empty. For a second I couldn't decide if this was good or bad. My mind just wanted to shut down or at least go back to the comforting rhythm of thud-swish-bang.

I thought maybe the students were possibly hiding out back behind the Auxiliary Gym, an area not easily viewed from the rest of the school. A likely hiding place if ever there was one. I spun on one heel and headed off toward the back of the school.

I blinked a little as I entered the cross hall that led to the back of the school. This cross hall for some reason had been given a double dose of lights when the school was refurbished a few years before I arrived.

I slowed my pace a little as I got near the doors at the end of the hallway. If there were kids out there I didn't want them to hear my heels, although I wasn't one hundred percent sure anyone in the vicinity wouldn't be able to hear my heart thudding away.

When I was in grade school the Principal wore the loudest shoes in the world and we could always hear her coming. As soon as everyone heard the loud clacking of her heels on the Kent tile floor of the hallway we all headed back for our assigned spaces knowing that once there, we were safe from punishment. After all, we all knew you couldn't be punished if you followed the rules, right?

The Principal, Sister Marie, nicknamed Sister Elephante', had a rather thin physique with oversized, elephantine calves. They were huge and their weight combined with the harsh heeled shoes she wore made for some loud clacking when she came down the hall toward a noisy, out of control classroom.

I always wondered how such a seemingly intelligent woman could never figure out how it was we always knew she was coming. I can remember thinking to myself that if I were ever a principal I would have smarts enough to wear silent shoes.

The genius of Sister Elephante' was, of course, that she knew exactly what was going on. Her hall banging shoes were like a lion's roar. She got the whole herd moving to where she wanted, without having to lift a paw to punish anyone.

Sister Elephante' skillfully avoided conflict while I, like a dolt, was sneaking up to the back doors looking for a fight. I hugged the left side of the hallway so that I wouldn't be visible to anyone standing lookout. As I inched up the last few feet I got a good look at the outside. There was nothing. Just a half empty parking lot that stretched a few hundred yards to the old football field.

My whole face started to radiate heat as soon as I saw the emptiness. I was humiliated, angry and panicked all at once. I paused and took a deep breath in the hope that a solution would bubble to the surface. And then it came, the thought I was desperate for: the cafeteria!

I headed out across the parking lot to the side door of the cafeteria. It was my last and only hope. The students on both floors in the classrooms that faced the back of the campus would be watching so I resisted the temptation to run to the cafeteria. I went back to thud-swish-bang; although, the bangs were now muted somewhat by the macadam of the parking lot.

I took the stairs leading to the cafeteria doors two at a time because if I walked up slowly, anyone in the cafeteria on the lookout for an administrator would see my head appearing over the horizon of the window sill like the sails of a slow moving ship returning to port. It would give them ample time to skedaddle before I could get a look-see into the cafeteria.

I got to the door and grabbed the handle, yanked it open and slipped inside before anyone in the room could react. It would have been a beautiful moment had it not been for the screech of the hinges on the old door protesting my demand it move swiftly and the fact that the cafeteria was completely empty.

I blinked. I blinked again. I got a certain sinking feeling and a vague desire to lie down. I was finished. I was out of ideas. I was on the job for ten minutes and I had been outwitted by a group of seventh graders, every one an evil genius.

My feet suddenly felt very heavy. I knew I had to go back to my office and inform the principal. I stumbled toward the big blue doors at the back of the cafeteria. This was going to be an ugly conversation.

Then, just as I left the cafeteria, it hit me. I was, at that moment, pretty sure I had it figured out. I started to feel a huge sense of relief. I paused and took in a huge breath because I wasn't sure if I had been breathing since I discovered the deserted cafeteria.

I had checked all the obvious stuff then considered the not so obvious possibilities. I realized that maybe, in this instance, the problem was both the most obvious and the most unlikely: the teacher was wrong. Or, from another point of view, the teacher was a fucking idiot! You'd be amazed to know just how many of them are.

Then again, maybe you wouldn't. The students were not in Mr. Woods' classroom because they were not *supposed* to be in his classroom.

I headed back to my office and quickly ascertained that my hypothesis was correct. I got on the phone with Mr. Woods.

"Mr. Woods? Yeah, hi. The students are not in your class because they aren't supposed to be there."

"They're not?" he said with an air of surprise which told me he had never even considered that possibility.

"Yeah, this is day one and that particular class is only with you on days two, four and six."

"Oh," he said somewhat sheepishly.

"Yeah. It's all on the schedule we gave you in your teacher packet," I said, as a not so subtle means of telling him that this mistake was entirely his fault and the result of him not paying attention.

Blame is an interesting issue in schools. I am tempted to say that blame in schools is like a plague passed from one to another, finding a home in the host body with the lowest immune defenses. But it is more than a living entity looking for places to survive. It's more like a force of nature in schools.

As a force of nature, it follows immutable natural laws, the first of which is: anti-blame in sufficient quantity can completely cancel out blame. Everyone in the education system understands instinctively that with blame comes responsibility which may yield consequences. Therefore, a supply of anti-blame must be stored in sufficient quantity for any given happenstance.

It is logical to believe that fixing problems would be better than fixing blame but there are few in the system that do. One may rely on truth in such matters however; another immutable fact in the school universe is that blame is not always related to truth. Truth and blame may coexist, however they are linked, as often as not. Hence, blame can be a strong force as inescapable as the gravity of a black hole or a weak force easily deflected. All school administrators are keen blame deflectors.

"Oh," was all Mr. Woods said. What else could he say? He was hanging over a super big black hole of blame.

"Well they can be tricky to read," I said. "If you need anything else let me know. Talk to you later, bye."

My last comment to Mr. Woods was in effect saying, 'Hey buddy you are to blame for this mishap! It's not *my* fault. But although you have to take responsibility for this, there will be no consequences.' Resistance to blame can be, in most instances, easily reduced if the possibility of consequence is eliminated.

It was as if my head had two minds in it; one mind razor sharp and cynical, the other, dull and hopeful. I could switch between them and I often did.

In the sharp mind I saw every scam, every lie, every little bit of bullshit a mile off. I was able to calculate so quickly that it often seemed I could read minds. I knew what people were going to say and how they were going to say it before they said it.

In the dull mind I believed in people. I focused on their good qualities and if they had none I made them up. I told myself that their motives were purely in the interest of the students. In the dull mind every student had potential and none of them were criminal.

At first I would go to my dull mind for a few minutes to take a break. As time went on I spent more and more time there. Eventually, I couldn't tell which mind I was in or if it was the correct one for the given situation.

I must confess that I was a little proud of myself because of the way I deftly handled the force of blame. I was an administrator for all of approximately twenty minutes and I directed blame as any seasoned veteran could have. Looking back on it now, I know that I was more clueless than a truckload of guidance counselors.

I hung up the phone and mumbled "idiot" to myself not really sure to whom I was referring, him for not being able to read a simple schedule or me for letting him off the hook.

I slumped in my chair still sweaty from the ordeal. I felt heavy. Somehow gravity was exerting a greater force on me than it had twenty minutes ago. I started to mentally calculate how much more time I had left in the day when the phone rang. I reached for it immediately.

Chapter 3

"I talked to Dr. Mayonnaise yesterday. He wants us to up the penalty for fighting to ten days OSS," he said then paused, "Hey Harris you getting this?"

"Oh yeah," I said as I looked up from my pad. "I assumed you were pausing for dramatic effect."

I was in the Principal's office for our never scheduled but always occurring morning meeting. The building level administration at Sunnydale consisted of a Principal and two Assistant Principals. There was Principal Apple, myself and Rick Bird. Three administrators to run a school of a thousand inner-urban minority students with an almost impossible climb ahead of them to the American dream, and sixty five mutinous dogs commonly referred to as teachers.

My mind had been wandering and I had missed my cue to look obsequious and nod during his ramble. I could tell by his expression that he was mulling over whether or not I was making light *with* him or making light *of* him. I always got the feeling that his sense of humor and my sense of humor were like two trains passing on a bridge, they were close but they never connected.

Apple was the sort of person who needed to talk. I would go to lunch with him and he would talk endlessly about the women he'd conquered, the men he'd bested in business deals, the famous people he'd met and the pranks he'd pulled. I would listen to His Blowhardiness silently judging him while I marked how many times he had told whatever vignette he was on and how the story had changed since the last time he told it.

He was never dressed in a suit. He always wore sport coats which were all very large in order to cover his enormous stomach. His clothes were always wrinkled and seldom matched. The color combinations of his dress had the range in hue of a fruit salad that had been shoved into the back of an iron bladed fan and splattered onto a wall.

"Does he still want us to call the police?" I asked, interrupting his mental deliberations on my last statement. He probably would have filed my response in the wiseass file had I let him finish his thoughts on the matter. I probably would have too.

I was sitting with Rick across from Apple who sat leaning back behind his desk. Apple had a way of leaning back in his chair which made his considerable stomach seem even larger.

"Yeah, he also wanted me to remind you the new math teacher starts today."

"Oh yeah! Ms. Siren," I said in mock lasciviousness.

Apple and I laughed at that.

"I don't understand. What is so funny?" Rick asked.

"This is the girl I told you about. The really hot one. The only job candidate that ever got walked to the door by the Superintendent after the interview," I explained.

"Oh, I remember now."

Rick was in almost every way Principal Apple's opposite. He was a tall, thin, unassuming man of uncommon decency. He was efficient, hard working and I have no doubt that had he the inclination, he could have been a formidable blame deflector but he always accepted what came his way.

Rick was always well-dressed in the efficient but somewhat dull way a man whose wife picks out his clothes does. Whereas Apple dressed more like a hobo trying to look his best to get a free meal at a church on Thanksgiving, Rick dressed as if he was trying to impress conservative in-laws.

Both men were in their fifties. Just rounding forty, I was the youngest administrator. I always wore a nice tailored suit, silk tie, silk hanky and leather shoes with a mirror shine you could check your teeth with.

"She's the girl I was telling you about. The one who went to all those Christian schools, choir and such. She's a real holy roller," I said.

Rick nodded again in acknowledgement.

"She's hot," Apple said shaking his head slightly, looking wistful as if to imply he'd bed her himself if it weren't for his marriage, as if such a thing was possible.

"Yeah, she's a delicate little thing," I said choosing to ignore Apple's embarrassing demeanor.

"Maybe you'll get lucky," Apple said changing to a mocking grin which belied the statement which in turn made me want to hit him with a crowbar.

I smiled back at him as if to say, 'maybe,' but I had no intention of going after Ms. Siren. Besides already being married, I didn't want to get involved with someone I worked with. If things go sour, and up till then every relationship I'd ever had with a woman besides my wife, did, I would have to see her every day. Also, going after a subordinate, however hot she may be can get you fired. That would be worse than a million guidance counselors *not* being killed.

Still, I couldn't help but notice that Ms. Siren was hot. She had round brown eyes you could swim in and a perfectly shaped, petit body that looked as if it would break if touched. Were circumstances different, I would have loved to take her for a few laps around the track.

"What else did the Superintendent have to say?" Rick asked.

"He wants us to make sure we get ready for the state tests next month," Apple said. "Harris?"

"I'm on it. I already met with the teachers and the staff and have worked out a basic strategy."

"Mr. Hadley complained there were kids running around upstairs after the lunch cycle," Apple said.

"I'll try to get up there but I'll tell Stubby to patrol there after sixth period," I replied.

Apple asked, "How's he been doing?"

"Okay so far."

"He started with us just at the end of last year," Apple said.

"The school board hired him," Rick said

in a tone which told me he didn't approve.

"Do they do that a lot here?" I asked.

"They do it enough," Apple retorted.

Rick was about to say something then caught himself. What was he about to say before he stopped himself? I didn't ask. Perhaps the sharp mind sent a message over to the dull mind threatening to stab it if it was so stupid as to ask.

"Just remember," Apple said, "Lou Mustard is not only the president of the school board he's also a snake. Don't trust him."

"I'll keep it in mind," I said, not a little shocked at his candor.

"You'd better," Rick said, rising to go back to his office.

I rose too and walked back to my office. Our offices were laid out in a line like a railroad flat. Looking at the arrangement as a whole it seemed as if the offices themselves were an afterthought. The main office had two doors separated by a large bank of mailboxes which opened toward the main hallway. There was a narrow strip of floor between the doors and a high, heavy oak counter that ran the length of the office. It was a giant barrier to the small area that served as the office work space.

There was just enough room for the two secretaries' desks and a copy machine. The three principals' offices were in a row and the walls for my office, which as the new guy I was required to take because it was closest to the office doors, seemed to start in the middle of the main office. It was a tight affair.

As I got to my office door, I could see the morning rush in the office was just heating up. Biffy, the secretary Rick and I shared, was sitting at her desk reading a magazine. She rarely worked and she didn't have to. Her mother, who worked in the district office, was having an affair with the

President of the School Board. Lending weight to the adage frequently used by my Uncle Mike, "It's not who you know but who you blow."

I sat at my desk and started to push some papers around when I heard someone at my door say, "Hello?"

The man at the door had a full head of white hair, round rimless glasses and a thick white mustache. He had a kindly look which matched his melodious voice. He was either a grandparent looking to get a lunch to a forgetful grandchild or an Alzheimer's patient who wandered away from whatever goofatorium they had him shelved in.

"Hello," I said.

He entered, walked over to my desk and shook my hand. I did the same thing I do every time I shake hands; I instantly made a mental note to wash my hands as soon as possible.

"Harris Farmer, Assistant Principal with

the heart of gold."

"Don White, substitute teacher," he said smiling.

Substitute Teacher? This old guy as a substitute teacher in a modern school? I didn't know whether to laugh or cry.

"Well it's a pleasure to meet you. You're going to be a music teacher for today. Do you know anything about music? It's okay if you don't."

"Oh yeah, I play the guitar. I played in a band when I was in high school," he said.

High School? When the hell was that?

The whole time we were talking I was edging out the office door and toward the main office doors. He instinctively followed me and we continued the conversation.

Sunnydale was well maintained and, were this a Hollywood movie, given the complexion of our student body; there would be graffiti on the walls and rap music playing in the background. But there was no graffiti on the walls. Nor was there loud rap music playing.

The main hallway was flush with nearly the entire student body milling about and conversing. They were mostly minority students, all devotees of the gangster rapper style. Despite their desperate desire to look menacing, they were mostly harmless kids doing all the things kids have been doing in high schools since high school was invented. All their behaviors were underwritten with the most timeless of beliefs, that their rebellion was somehow different from all the other teenage rebellion that preceded it.

"I played in a band when I was in high school," he repeated.

He obviously thought I didn't hear him due to the din in the hallway which was considerable to the uninitiated.

"Good."

"Yeah, I have a 1964 Fender Jaguar."

"Wow, a '64 Jaguar. That is one of the finest guitars ever made." I wasn't shining him on. Gramps had a classic instrument.

"I bought it when I was in high school."

"What color?"

"It's brown," he practically shouted over the growing noise as we made our way to the music suite through the conversing students.

"Like a starburst?" I asked. I didn't have to yell. Unlike his voice, mine is not soft and it carries well in all environments. A voice like mine is one hell of an asset in a school setting but I have been accused of shouting in many non-school environments when I was doing nothing of the sort.

"Why?"

"They made a Foam Green version which is a real collector's item and my personal favorite. They changed the neck on that model. It's the first guitar Fender offered with 22 frets. Made it longer. Great sound. Either way you have one hell of a guitar."

"Do you play the guitar?" he asked trying to make sense of my knowledge on the subject.

"A little. Mostly I memorize esoteric facts of no particular value."

"Really?"

"Cogitae Ergo Sum."

"What?"

"Exactly!" I said, just as we entered the main lobby. "Let me walk you to the music suite. I'll unlock it for you."

We worked our way down the hall which was becoming more crowded. Hall traffic always peaked five minutes before the first bell. After that, students tended to drift off to class. There were always the slowpokes and the legitimately late whose lockers all started slamming on cue at the first bell.

When we got about halfway down the hall we ran into Eddie Angle. He was a muscular man-child in his mid forties whom I believe was purposely made stupid by God to spare him the pain of knowing what an ass he was. Still, I got along with him, mostly because I pitied him.

Eddie was a graduate of Sunnydale and a mediocre basketball player on a championship team back in the seventies. His whole life was the school sports program. He had wrangled a job making seven dollars an hour working as an aide for the emotional support class. Quite an accomplishment for one so dumb.

"Hey Mr. Farmer."

"Hey Mr. Angle. Mr. Angle, meet Mr. White. Mr. White is going to be a substitute teacher for us."

"Hello," White said with a nod.

"Nice to meet ya."

"Mr. Angle is our aide in the Emotional Support class. Next to me he's the nicest guy at Sunnydale."

"Yeah right," Eddie said with a chuckle.

We continued down the hall to the cross hall that led to the music suite. The number of students in this area was small, mostly because instead of lockers, this area had huge glass cases stuffed with the bona fides of Sunnydale's better days. Miss Nickels was just coming in from the parking lot. She was late as usual.

Technically, she wasn't late but she was in her early fifties and the size of a small garage. Moving all that bulk was a slow process. She'd never make it to her class on time.

The truly remarkable thing about Miss

Nickels was that her sister, the home economics teacher, was even larger than she. Neither one of them ever married. I speculated that they sublimated food for sex. Of course, that was a speculation I had no intention of investigating.

"Hey Miss Nickels"

"Howdy Mr. Farmer. How you be doin?"

"Better, now that I know you're here. Hey, this is Mr. White he's going to be a substitute here. Mr. White, this is Miss Nickels. She teaches Social Studies when she isn't sexually harassing me."

"Nice to meet you"

"It's nice to meet ya. Don't you be minding him. He always be funnin."

Just then Ms. Siren strode in from the parking lot. I could read her mind. She was thinking, 'Oh shit, the one time I'm running late and there's an administrator right there.' I made a mental note to make a note of it in my daily journal.

I know it sounds cruel or snarky to record such a thing, but it was my job and if there is one thing I learned, it's that records are important. I could stand at the door and watch a certain employee show up to work late everyday but the minute I *say* that employee has a problem with arriving to work on time I will be told that it is only my opinion. However, if I write it down, my "opinion" is magically transformed into something acceptable.

"I don't know if you remember me from your initial interview," I said to Ms. Siren as she approached. "I'm Harris Farmer, Assistant Principal Fact Totem. This here is my loyal substitute teacher Mr. White."

"Hi," she said with an expansive smile that radiated cute at a near lethal dosage.

"Nice to meet you."

"I'm going to open the music suite for my man here then I'll stop by to see how everything is going."

"Okay."

Mr. White and I continued on.

"She's new here too."

"She's a very attractive young lady," he said.

"Really? I hadn't noticed. This is the music suite. You shouldn't have any problems. Our students look and sound scary but they are really very good kids. However, I suggest you don't show fear. Just kidding. I will be by a few times during the day. I always act like the substitute and I are old friends so that it doesn't seem I am checking on you or them. Just play along. Okay?"

"Okay."

"Just remember to take careful attendance

and if there's a fire alarm, close the windows and doors and take the student list with you. If you get into any trouble hit the call button near the door and an administrator will be here before you can say "panic." But don't say it . . . and don't do it. This'll be a piece of cake. Any questions?"

"No, ah. . . I don't think so."

"Good, I gotta get back to it."

The look of uncertainty on his face was spreading quickly to the rest of his body. I had about two seconds to come up with something inspirational to give this Doughboy the courage to go over the top.

I said, "Not to worry my good man, if you don't make it, I'll personally see to it the Jaguar gets a good home."

"Thanks," he said smiling.

I walked away, leaving him to his fate.

Chapter 4

My sometime secretary, Biffy, informed me that the sometimes competent Mr. Woods wanted to see me. I went down to the woodshop. It was the only classroom at Sunnydale that wasn't in the building proper. It was in a building connected to the main building by a glass breezeway. The difficulty for me was that the district office was just across the hall from the woodshop.

I had received several complaints from the women who worked in the district office about the noise from the woodshop. Mr. Woods was the sort of teacher who couldn't control a class. His Holiness, the Superintendent, called me into his office to tell me to take care of the matter personally.

There is not a more dishonest, treacherous group of prevaricators than superintendents. If a superintendent tells you that you are living on Earth, you would be wise to double check what planet you're on. About the only thing they will be honest with you about is that which they do not like or want. And they don't like to hear that you couldn't get done what they asked you to get done.

I assumed the reason Mr. Woods wanted to see me was because he was having a problem with a student or possibly students. Perhaps, he needs me to come down and tell him what day of the week it is.

When I got there his room was empty of students and he was at his desk located in the front corner of the room opposite the door. It abutted one of the two heavy oak work tables along the high window sill. He'd placed his desk as far away from the ten or so student desks, which occupied the center of the room, as he could and still qualify as being in the room.

"You needed something Mr. Woods?" I asked as I entered.

"Yeah, I never see any administrators and these kids all act like animals," he practically shouted at me.

"Animals eh?"

"Yes, and you guys don't back me up," he said as he jumped up and started waving his arms.

"What would you suggest?" I asked in a level voice.

Blaming the poor quality of the students and the lassitude of the administrators for his failures is a classic strategy of his sort. I'd seen it many times.

When I served as a sign language interpreter I essentially worked with the same group of students throughout the school day. I watched as the same thirty kids, paired with my three deaf students, became a totally different group in each class. In one class they worked diligently and were respectful, in another class they were rowdy and troublesome, in yet still another they were compliant but disinterested in participating. It was clear to me then that the teacher's ability to control and motivate a class had much to do with the students' behavior.

I could explain that to Woods for a thousand years and he would still come back with how it was everybody else's fault. The kids were kids, not animals. And the administrators were administrators, not wizards. We don't have the power to control a class from the outside nor is it our responsibility to do so, but try telling that to Sir Whines-a-lot.

"You guys don't care! You just sit in your office and don't do anything! Every time I look away they throw something at me! I can't let them work with the machines because they don't follow the safety rules! This is crazy-,"

"Mr. Woods please calm yourself," I interrupted, hoping to short circuit his anger spiral. "I am willing to do anything to help you but you should know that discipline in schools has to start in the classroom. I cannot impose discipline from outside your class."

But I was committing a rookie mistake. The dirtiest word in all of Education is "No." The best-case scenario is to say "no," without the person you're saying "no," to recognizing that you just told them "no." Or to put it another way: to convince someone that the answer is "yes" when it is in fact "no" is the Acme of skill.

Woods got even more upset. His face turned three shades of pissed off and he repeated everything he'd said since I entered the room again only slightly faster and slightly louder.

Realizing that I had screwed up by being honest with him I tried another tack. I tried to redirect his focus for a moment.

"Mr. Woods let me ask you, what have you been covering in class?"

"I've been covering measurement. I can't do anything else with them," he said, as he started rooting through the papers on his desk. He found what he was looking for and handed it to me.

I took a look at it and I was stunned. It was a worksheet that looked as if it had been the last in a line of ten thousand copies of a copy. It was faded with a bunch of spots and scratches accumulated through the numerous generations that came before it. The content of the worksheet was easily the most boring piece of school work left over from the 1950s.

I almost couldn't believe what I was seeing. This clueless bastard actually managed to make shop class less fun than a root canal on Christmas day. I had a strong urge to throw something at him. However, I tried to go easy on him.

"Perhaps you could make the class more interactive."

"What do you mean?" he asked.

"It's just that I think the expectations of students when they come to shop class are different than what you've been doing."

"It doesn't matter! These kids are not going to behave no matter what I do. You haven't been here that long. You don't know these kids like I do. I've been here 16 years, nothing is going to work. I need an administrator to show up around here to help me."

My sharp mind did all of the calculations and determined that basically, Mr. Woods is incapable of doing his job and is claiming that it is the fault of me and the other administrators. I couldn't imagine how he had to mangle logic before he could conclude that I or any principal would go along with that. Stupid plus boring divided by an inability to reason equals a no win scenario.

"Mr. Woods I hear what you're saying. I will make sure I get down here at least a few times each morning. Assuming of course nothing else comes up. Okay?"

"Okay," he said and sucked in a deep breath which was both a sign he was finally placated, and an attempt to head off hyperventilation. He wiped the beaded sweat from his forehead with a handkerchief he whipped from his back pocket.

The truth is, I would do as I said but I gave him a low priority. He was just looking to get me to do his work. He figures if I'm in the room the students will behave and he is correct for the most part, but as soon as I leave, they are back to business as usual with a little more mayhem thrown in as retaliation for bringing an administrator into it.

The whole deal was a play within a play.

Of course the students will behave when the discipline is external. The trick, and the goal, is to educate them to exercise internal control. Any teacher can keep the students in their seats and quiet by placing a gun to their heads but how much learning will go on? How healthy is that?

There are a million things that play into the student-teacher relationship. If it goes sour because the teacher is a jerk, any class can quickly devolve into guerilla warfare with the teacher calling in more and more air-strikes while the insurgency commits more and more raids.

In my experience, choice is a huge factor in human compliance. If people, and it should always be remembered that students are people, feel they are participants in the decisions made about them they are more likely to cooperate.

When I was a student teacher in a school very much like Sunnydale I heard a young female student in the back of the room yell, "No that's mine! Hey he took my chair! I was sitting there!" I went to the back of the class to appraise the situation.

In the back of the room was the kid. The kid the last student teacher warned me about. The one he said was pure evil and to watch out for.

I wasn't happy about being the second student teacher in the first quarter of the school year. The students, having experienced the coming and going of the student teacher before me, I felt, would be less likely to behave. They would be hip to the fact that no matter how little they cooperated I would be leaving in a few weeks.

But there he was. And there I was, one scared student teacher. Fortunately for me I inherited a little of the non commissioned officer genes from my father. Genes which said: never show fear, and in a crisis situation, start doing, even if you don't know what to do.

I could see he was sitting on a chair in the rear of the classroom where I had sent the students to do some group project I dreamed up. The indignant girl was standing with her arms akimbo and a look of fury on her face. She looked at me and complained, "He took my chair!"

I looked at the kid who seemed to be bracing for a fight. Be it verbal or physical I could not tell. He was sitting in the chair with his arms crossed contracting all the muscles in his body as if he were trying to make himself heavier in the way children do in the mistaken belief such a thing is possible.

I looked at him and surprised both him and me by asking, "Do you want to give her the chair?"

"No," he said firmly.

I turned to the girl and said, "Get another chair."

Before she could react, the classroom terrorist jumped out of his chair and said, "No, no, she can have this one."

I said, "Okay, now we have the chair thing settled let's get to work."

I could tell you that kid was just looking for a fight and when I didn't give it to him he backed down, but I don't believe that is what happened. He was testing me as much as he was protesting.

He knew I could make him give up the chair. I could have called in an air strike and had him removed from class but instead I offered him a choice. I let him decide if he wanted the chair. It was never about the chair for him. He hated being a powerless kid always being acted upon by the system and he wanted to rattle the bars a little to get back.

I had inadvertently turned the tables on him. By treating him with respect he had not the will to disrespect me. He was my best student after that. And as corny as it sounds that "crazy kid," the one Mr. Woods would surely identify as an "animal," taught me a great lesson.

The problem was, I couldn't figure out a way to teach that lesson to Woods. I don't know if he was capable of learning anything but he sure wasn't up to the task today.

I nodded to Mr. Woods and smiled slightly. He nodded back. The bargain struck, I made my exit and headed down to the cafeteria for the first lunch.

Though loud, the cafeteria is one of my favorite places in school. I guess that's because it is one of the few places I see students happy. It is a parade without music, however, since the food is purely heinous, a caustic combination of animal fat and cheese. It's the place good food goes when it dies. Oh, and in case you were wondering, the reason school cafeterias can serve leftovers indefinitely is because the food is so vile that even bacteria won't touch it; consequently, it never spoils.

I usually stood next to the main doors to the cafeteria because it gave me the best view into the kitchen area as well as the cafeteria itself. I was a pro at lunch duty. I had been assigned lunch duty every year I was a teacher.

Sunnydale was the only school I ever worked in where the teachers demanded an administrator be present at lunch. It was also the only school I had ever served in where the teachers were paid extra to do lunch duty, a circumstance so perplexing to me I have yet to figure out how it ever came about.

"Hey Farmer, whatsup?"

I looked down to see Alejandro Sanchez approaching. He was a small 14 year old ninth grader with cerebral palsy. Alejandro walked with a pronounced limp shuffle. He was always an upbeat kid but he had an unfortunate habit of fighting with the other students.

He reached out and we shook hands in the elaborate fashion the students of Sunnydale had developed for themselves. Even though I detested shaking hands I did find something comical in this ritual and I never let on that shaking hands was something I'd rather not do.

"Mr. Farmer," I corrected.

"Mr. Farmer, right. How you doin?"

"Okay today. How's things with you, Alejandro?" I said, deliberately pronouncing the "j" sound. "What's with the Mets shirt? Oh, I guess your Yankee shirt is in the wash. Or is this embarrass-your-parents day here at Sunnydale?"

He laughed, "Mr. Farmer you whack!"

"If by 'whack' you mean young, intelligent and incredibly well dressed, then yes, I am whack. Quite whack."

He started to move off. I said, a little more serious but not harshly, "Hey Alejandro," pronouncing his name correctly this time. "No fights today okay? If I have to call your mom with any more bad news she's gonna have a hit man out looking for me."

"Okay Mr. Farmer," he said and shuffled off.

"Hey Mr. Farmer!" said a bright voice.

It was Torquisha. She was a pleasant girl with a sad home life. Like so many students I dealt with over the years, she didn't have any one problem that couldn't be solved by stuffing both her parents in a trash compactor, flipping the switch and then ordering a decent set from the Brady Bunch catalogue.

She had every reason to be bitter but she was not. I liked her because I wanted to be more like her. I am nowhere near as upbeat and, were I in her difficult shoes, I'd be ten times the pain in the ass any one of Sunnydale's students could ever claim to be. She was a special individual. The trick was getting her to see that.

"Torki! How you doin'?" I said smiling a genuine smile.

"Good."

"Glad to hear it. They said you were going to buy me lunch today on account of it being Buy-Your-Principal-Lunch-Day."

"Aw Mr. Farmer you know I ain't got no money. For real," she said beaming, but not quite sure if I was teasing.

"What? With all that babysitting you do? C'mon now."

"Mr. Farmer you know I just be babysitting for my brothers and sisters. My momma don't gimme no money fo dat."

"You've got talent kid. It's worth more than money. Besides I made up that stuff about

Buy-Your-Principal-Lunch-Day."

"Mr. Farmer you just be trying to git me," she said shaking her head and moving off toward the snaking line that disappeared into the kitchen door.

"I know! It's whack. You enjoy your lunch."

As she moved away, Stubby entered through the main doors. He gave her a long look and nodded to Torquisha as if to say "hey." He then turned, walked over to me and took up a guard position adjacent to mine.

"Hey Mr. Farmer, what you be doin'?"

"Hey Mr. Stubby. Just watching the lunch crowd. Occasionally being whack."

"Tsh, yeah."

"I was also wondering why they call you Stubby when you don't appear to be very stubby to me. I mean, like, what are you, six-two?"

"Six-three. My moms call me dat when I was a baby. Everybody call me dat."

"Mother eh? I had a mother."

Stubby was indeed a large man. He was wall to wall muscles. He kept his head shaved clean and his ultra dark skin contrasted so much with the palms of his hands that I couldn't help but stare at them when he motioned as he talked.

Stubby was a keen student of human nature and as such he never resorted to intimidation to gain the students' compliance. I often wished many of our allegedly college educated teachers had his insight and ability with students.

"I was the baby. I got six brothers."

"Six brothers!? Your poor mother. On the other hand, two more children and you guys would have had enough for a baseball team. I guess she was just a quitter, huh?"

"Nah, she just never liked baseball," he said smiling.

"What do all your brothers do? Do you see them at all now that you're all grown up?"

"Nah I don't see them much, they all in prison."

"All in prison?"

"Yeah we be from the ghetto. My one brother he be getting twenty years."

"Twenty years, wow. What'd he do?" Then, realizing that my question might offend I hastily added, "If you don't mind my asking."

I have had to deal with the unfortunate circumstance of having a curious nature and a desire to learn. It is a combination which pretty much pisses people off. I was always getting in trouble in religious school when I was a kid because I asked questions. I suppose I can understand religious people, whose goal is to inculcate dogma, perceiving questions as a threat to their mission but I could never figure out why the professors at college and graduate school got so angry with me for it.

In my mind it is perfectly acceptable to ask a question such as the one raised here because it is on point. Human interaction is far too complicated for such a simplistic view and even though I know that, I have often asked a question which I should not have. One of the few benefits of being me is that you get *real* good at apologizing.

"He be sellin drugs and doin shit."

"Sorry to hear that Stubby," I said, scanning the faces of the students at the tables nearest us to determine if any of them heard him use the s-word.

"It's aright. That happen a lot where we grew up. That's why I moved out-a-dere."

"Yeah, I can understand that."

Just then two students started horsing around. One of them stood up on his chair. Before I could even start over there Stubby took a step forward from our perch along the wall and yelled, "Yo! Yo! Yo! Eh! Y'all siddown now!"

All the noise in the cafeteria stopped. Every student not previously paying attention started swinging their heads scanning the room for the show. All were alerted to the matter. They had heard Stubby yell.

The student on the chair smiled and gave a small wave at Stubby as if to say, in the vernacular of the students, 'my bad,' then jumped back down into his seat. The crowd waited just long enough, approximately a millisecond, to see if either Stubby or I were going to go over to the offender and add a sequel to the show. When neither of us moved they turned back to their business and the noise resumed.

I wouldn't have handled the situation that way. I would have walked over to the student and said, "Could you get down off the chair please?" Then when the student got down I would probably say, "Thank you. Please don't do that again I don't want to see you get hurt."

I always said please and thank you with students. I never yelled the way Stubby had. It wasn't my style, but then you might ask why such a hostile and confrontational method worked for Stubby? The reason was because every student in that room knew him and had already formed the opinion that he was a decent person.

Students want to know if you are just another hostile adult in a hostile world or if you are someone who will benefit them. If they believe you do work in their interest, they will give you a great deal of leeway.

In all the years I worked in schools I have always liked the students better than the adults.

The students can drive you crazy with their antics but I have not found them to be any more offensive than the adults on the whole. The greatest characteristic of the students is their capacity to forgive and forget. The adults simply cannot do that.

It wasn't that Stubby, with his statuesque muscularity, was intimidating. The truth is, of the two of us, I was the scarier looking man. The combination of my mother's rounded looks and my father's angular configuration left me with a slightly protruding brow ridge, high cheek bones and a mid-sized nose that flared at the bottom. All this had the effect of a perpetual angry scowl. I was often assumed to be angry even when I was in a rare good mood.

The truth is, my understated tones, use of please and thank you combined with my Frankenstein facial features scared the hell out of students. Often, after getting to know me, students would say something like, "You really are a nice guy," in a way that expressed surprise.

Stubby didn't get respect because he was black like most of the students, including the one standing on the chair. It is a common misconception among blacks and whites that black people will be more amenable to black people than white people. That belief is a subtle prejudice based on the conviction that black people are of a kind and therefore of one mind. They are not.

Stubby got respect and compliance from the students because he earned it. In the complicated computations of schoolyard economics, Stubby was a bargain. He wasn't abusive nor was he a threat to well-being. He could also be quite helpful. I liked him for pretty much the same reasons.

Stubby waited, eyes fixed on the perpetrator for just long enough for him to know he had done wrong, then stepped back to his previous position at my side.

"Well said Mr. Stubby."

Chapter 5

The end of the day was my favorite time of day because here too, the students were happy. I loved to stand outside the school and watch them leave. Even the kids who had crappy homes, and we had many of those, seemed to take on a light-hearted air as they left the burden of school behind them. Yet, ironically, my prime motivation for standing outside at the end of the day at Sunnydale was to prevent fights.

Still, I always rushed through the last minute stuff so I could go out and watch the show. It put me in a good mood for the afternoon work which often stretched into the early evening and sometimes late evening. My work day at Sunnydale was a minimum ten hours with no breaks and most of the time, no lunch.

The main office just after the last bell is as chaotic as it is in the morning, perhaps more so because the teachers don't avoid it as they do in the morning when an administrator might take notice of their tardiness.

I was at the front counter rifling through my mail making sure there wasn't anything from the district office or the Emperor himself which needed immediate attention. Biffy was sitting at her desk diligently avoiding work by cutting pictures out of a magazine for reasons known but to God. The noise of fifty conversations going at once banged back and forth between the hard plaster walls. It encompassed every inch of the range of human hearing yet I managed to hear my name through the din.

"Mr. Farmer?"

I looked up and saw Markus, a scrawny eighth grader with a nearly shaved head. He was a polite child who loved and feared his mother in equal quantities. Who could blame him, half the time she scared me. He was a genuinely good student but we both knew that one phone call from me and his mother would "*whoop* him good."

"Markus! Ay, how you doin'?"

"Okay. I was wondering if I could have my phone back. Remember you said to come by at the end of the day?"

"That's right I did."

I happened to still have it in my pocket. I took it during fourth period and hadn't had long enough between crises to put it in my special electronics holding area. I pulled it out and held it up.

"You know Markus, this is a remarkable phone. I used it to call my friend who works for the Peace Corps in Africa and it sounded like he was standing right next to me!"

Markus' eyes grew wide. The conversations gradually tapered off as the crowd took interest in this exchange.

"It was amazing. We talked for like three hours and the connection didn't cut out once. You're a lucky kid to have such a fine phone."

He was thoroughly stunned and said, in a low voice that made it sound like he was talking to himself mostly, "That's gonna use up my minutes."

"Really? I hadn't thought of that. Oh well," I handed him the phone. "You have a good afternoon."

Markus took the phone, his mind reeling. "Thank you," he mumbled as he shuffled out.

The room had grown absolutely silent by the time Markus reached for his phone. Even Biffy had stopped what she was doing to watch. I had played my part so deadpan that she and the teachers weren't sure if I had actually called Africa with a confiscated cell phone.

The door closed behind Markus. I stared

at it for a beat as if in deep contemplation and continuing with my deadpan delivery I turned to the teachers and said, "That was cruel. I shouldn't have done that."

The room exploded in laughter as I headed back to my office to drop off my mail. They were still laughing a minute later when I headed out the door for the back of the school.

Sunnydale had a bus loop in the front of the school but the Superintendent forbade us to use it. All the buses and most of the departing students left the side of the building which was opposite the side with the woodshops and district office. I suspected Heir Superintendentoppengruppenfurhrer wanted to make sure the leaving students and any difficulties associated with their liberation were as far from his lying eyes as possible. After all, wasn't getting away from students one of the sweetest perks of the superintendency?

Dr. Mayonnaise was typical of superintendents in my experience. He was tall, handsome, polished, marginally intelligent and utterly ruthless. And I believe if he hadn't been manufactured in a factory, he would step over his own mother if it suited his desires.

He always wore double breasted suits and tried to talk me into getting a few but I didn't think it was a good look for me. He was slim and muscular with rounded shoulders and a double breasted suit looked good on him. I was thin and had broad shoulders which were accented by the double breasted jacket making me seem huge. That coupled with my hideous face made me seem even more monster-like.

In addition to the usual character flaws endemic to superintendents, Dr. Mayonnaise had one other problem; he was an ex-Art teacher. By the time I got to Sunnydale I had taught every subject, including art. I appreciate its value to education, it's just that specialty teacher's like art, music and foreign languages are clueless when it comes to discipline issues. They mostly teach students who have an affinity for what they teach and are often more enthusiastic about the subject matter. Thus the students in those classes tend to be less problematic. The kids who would give you a hard time because they don't want to be there, aren't there.

But even if Dr. Mayonnaise had been a real teacher with a real understanding of the day to day workings of a classroom, it wouldn't have mattered much. He was all for himself. He had the survival instincts of an alley cat and half the morals.

I headed down the main hallway to the side doors just beyond the Gym and the Auditorium. Sunnydale was essentially one long, two-level corridor with the ancillary stuff like the library, the cafeteria, the gym and the auditorium attached to it at various angles.

When I got outside I was refreshed to see that it was a classic fall day, my favorite kind. The sunlight bounced off of everything brightly, highlighting the panoply of colors in the trees. The air had a cool zing to it that worked itself nicely against the warmth of the sun. It was comfortable.

I saw Stubby standing at the far end of the building near the front yard of the school and I walked over to him.

"Ah Mr. Stubby, nothing so graced this school day like the leaving it."

"Huh? Yeah."

"What do you say we take a walk to the edge of our domain?"

"Sure."

There were three sets of double doors at the entrance to the Gym/Auditorium lobby.

Outside the doors was a sort of bus loop. On the other side of the loop was a staircase that led down to a rather large parking lot. The lot tended to seem larger than it really was because it never had more than eight cars in it. Most of our students were too poor to afford cars and most of them lived close enough to walk to school. Sunnydale ran a total of two busses.

Stubby and I started walking down the road that led off the bus loop in the front of the school to the side edge of the property as the last bus pulled away from the curb and headed out. There were several cars coming from the unused bus loop in the front of the school passing us as we walked.

The first three cars that passed us hit their horns and someone inside yelled out 'Stubby!" Just as we got to the edge of the property a blue shitmobile stopped and Stubby ran over to it. He conversed with the driver for a few seconds, shook his hand then strode back to where I was standing.

"You are a popular man Mr. Stubby."

"Yeah I was a football star when I went to Spartanburg High."

"Oh Yeah? What position did you play?"

"I was a running back. I made all state and got me a scholarship to Penn State. But I dropped out."

"What happened?"

"Couldn't do da school work. I jist didn't learn enough in high school."

"That's too bad. You think you could have gone pro were it not for that?"

"I don't know but I jist couldn't do da work. Probly spent too much time playing ball and chasing girls instead of learnin when I was in school."

"Women! Is there anything we won't do for them?"

Stubby laughed. "Yeah, I hear dat!"

Chapter 6

The experts say if a shark bites you, it is probably just trying to feel you with its teeth. Feel you. Not so much a taste as a sense of what you are.

That little bit of knowledge kept crossing my mind my first few weeks on the job. I kept feeling as if everyone were feeling me out with mouths full of razor sharp teeth. And if my thoughts on this matter were in any way accurate, the shark with the biggest teeth, the grand daddy with the biggest jaws, the Great White, if you will, was the school board.

If there is one thing I have learned about school boards from my years in education it's that if the school board thinks you are doing a good job, or if they think you are doing a bad job, you are.

Almost no school board members have ever taught so much as one class at any level. Of all the persons charged with running a school they are by far the least knowledgeable.

The board members at Sunnydale were among the dumbest of the dumb. Not one of them ever bothered to get a college degree and only half graduated high school. I frequently speculated as to how many of them could spell the word 'school.' I figured no more than one third. It was a conservative estimate.

They were constantly giving suggestions and issuing orders that were ridiculous. The most bizarre had to be when one school board member wanted me to suspend the entire eighth grade for acts of sabotage that allegedly took place while under the supervision of a substitute teacher.

The story was unfounded. The school board member had heard it from 'someone,' i.e. a disgruntled, misinformed teacher, that the room was torn apart, etc. Even though the story was total bullshit it took some work to redirect the board's focus from my suspending the entire eighth grade to something real.

The one thing school boards do focus on is hiring. School districts employ a plethora of methods when hiring. The oldest and most used trick is to have a "hiring committee." The committee approach is used most often because it spreads out the blame should the hiree turn out to be a dud, or a criminal, or both.

If the superintendent were to submit a person for hire without using a hiring committee and that new employee went south, then the superintendent would get all the blame and may have to take responsibility. Man, you better believe they don't want any part of that!

By involving a committee of teachers, board members and others, the superintendent can always say if things don't work out, 'I don't know what happened, everyone on the hiring committee was sure this person would have worked out.' What could anybody say to that?

Use of the committee dodge did not, however, prevent superintendents from hiring who they wanted for a particular position. The committee came to a decision as to whom to hire but it was the superintendent or his loyal toady, the assistant superintendent, who decided which applicants were granted an interview.

Superintendents often employ a tactic I call funneling. They choose, say, five candidates, four of whom are absolutely unhirable for a variety of reasons, the more varied the better, and one good candidate. It isn't hard for a superintendent to steer the committee to the "right" choice.

I had a friend who sat through a forty-five minute interview at the end of which it was determined that as a Science teacher, he probably wouldn't be right for the position of English teacher. Apparently, the copies of his certification and his job application which had "Science teacher" written all over them were "overlooked" by "somebody." But that didn't matter, he simply *couldn't* be hired. After all, he didn't have the proper certification.

If you are up for a job in a school district and one of your competition is related to someone on the school board, you aren't getting the job. Half the teachers at Sunnydale were in some way related to the school board. I called them "The Untouchables."

Dr. Mayonnaise didn't stand for much but he would not have the school board involved in the interviewing process. He was afraid that they would say or do something real stupid and cause a lawsuit. He was probably right in that.

I faced a hiring committee of administrators when I applied to Sunnydale and I was told later that I was the best of the lot who interviewed. Curiously, I was also told by Principal Apple, that if they could have gotten a black administrator they would have hired that person over me regardless of quality. They searched everywhere and even went so far as to do some schmoozing but it was to no avail. They couldn't find a black administrator to work with inner city black kids. In an ironic twist so indicative of the bizarre state of race relations in America, nearly all the black administrators they talked to wound up working at wealthy, predominately white, suburban schools that were glad to have them as symbols of their nonbiased ways.

I was actually working on the job before I met anyone from the school board, a situation I later found out they resented. They, like nearly all school boards, placed a heavy hand on the hiring process and when Dr. Mayonnaise kept them from this particular hire, they got angry.

Not long after I was hired, and just before school started, I was in my office with Rick. He was showing me how to work the computer program that was used to control every aspect of the day to day school bureaucracy.

"In order for you to set the calendar you have to go to the-,"

"Go to wherever. Ha ha," a scratchy but soft toned voice interrupted.

Rick and I both looked up to see a short, balding black man with the largest sweater I'd ever seen stretched over a sumo sized gut. He was wearing 70's vintage aviator glasses that in combination with the belly, made his head look small.

He swayed over to a chair, leaned over it and put his hands on the back. It looked as if he were trying to take the pressure off his lower back from his cantilevered stomach.

"Hello Lou," Rick said amiably. "Lou, this is Harris Farmer. Harris, this is Lou Mustard, President of the School Board."

"Hi," I said getting up to shake his outstretched hand. "It's nice to meet you."

"Likewise."

"I have to go check on something. Good to see you again Lou," Rick said, and glided out the door before I could think of something to stop him.

"Yeah, Rick," Lou said breathing heavy from the exertion of shaking my hand.

"Would you like to sit down? You look kind of tired."

He nodded and moved around the chair and sat down as I went back to my chair.

"So, how do you like working here?"

"It's been nice so far."

"Glad to hear it but if that changes you let me know."

My sharp mind picked up the subtlety of what he had just said but my dull mind told me that I was wrong, no one would jump into such a proposal so quickly.

"Sure Lou, Is it okay if I call you Lou or would that offend you?"

"Lou is fine and you can call me if you need to tell me anything."

It was right then he was letting me know that he wanted me to pass him information without going through the Principal or the Superintendent. A snake indeed I decided, and in that instant, my sharp mind sent an I-told-you-so to my dull mind.

"Well, I'm sure the Principal and the Superintendent are pretty good about keeping you up to speed about what's going on."

"They don't tell me everythin'," he said almost defensively.

There's that gnawing sensation again, I thought. There was no way I was going to do what he was asking but the problem was how to get that across to him. I couldn't think of a better strategy than honesty. In my own defense I had only been a school administrator for a short while.

"Well I appreciate you letting me know. But I think what you're suggesting is unethical and I wouldn't feel right doing such a thing to the Principal or the Superintendent."

"You betta be remembering who you work for. Dere be consequences for not payin attention."

Was this guy serious? He was trying to intimidate me. I grew up in a rough, poverty-stricken neighborhood and I think that experience somehow has made me immune to intimidation.

Nevertheless, I remained pleasant when I said, "I'm sure there are. I just hope my work here is judged on its merits not politics. I'm not a politician."

There was a long moment when we just stared at each other. I smiled then he smiled. End of round one.

"Are you married?"

Back to small talk.

"One wife, several children. How about yourself?"

"I'm married, my son is a senior here," he said, shaking his head slightly. "How your marriage be doin?"

"It's fine enough but it consumes a great deal of free time and for those of us who have to buy the extra, extra large condoms, it can be expensive Lou."

He hesitated then laughed. He used the front of my desk to hoist himself to a standing position. "We gonna keep our eyes on you," he said, then waddled out.

I thought a great deal about that meeting. What the hell was going on with these people that the president of the school board would try to establish his own informant network like he was some Cold War KGB agent? How much intrigue could there be in a school that nobody outside of those directly involved could give a shit about?

It was also an incredibly thoughtless thing to do to someone who spent as many years as I had preparing for that job. But then, what would he know about how much work it took to become a principal? According to Dr. Mayonnaise, Lou flunked out of college his first semester.

In the American school system it is quite natural that I, a trained professional with three college degrees and many years of experience, should take my cues from a semi-literate college dropout who got his position by getting 41 people in his ward to vote for him.

Not a lot of registered voters in the Sunnydale district.

Chapter 7

"And this is Mrs. Scott," the superintendent said genially, as if we were on a game show rather than a job interview.

I nodded and smiled.

"I'm going to tell you a little about us then we're gonna have you tell us about yourself, then we're gonna ask you some questions. Okay?"

I nodded. He began telling me about the district but he wasn't talking to me. He was talking to the two board members who were on this hiring committee of nine. Nine people to scrutinize me.

I'd already sized up the school on my way in. They were rich and pompous. The school was the polar opposite of Sunnydale. They had all the advantages. Yet, for all the perks, the numerous academic trophies standing proudly in the trophy case next to the numerous sports trophies, and the titanic self esteem, I knew they were not nearly all they could be.

If I pointed out the places they needed improvement, they'd never hire me. I wasn't sure I wanted to be hired but a fast way to throw the interview would be to intimate that I would change things. People hate change and their thinking during an interview becomes positively reptilian. Each of the nine crocodiles I was presently facing, and had to swim past to be an administrator again, all had one overriding concern: 'How's hiring this guy gonna affect *me*?'

They'd make their decision most probably in the first two to four minutes. Not much time for someone who looks as unattractive as me. Those precious few moments would be like a day if I had the looks of a young Robert Redford but, alas, that is not the case.

Nevertheless, he finished his spiel and it

was my turn to talk. I told them of how I'd started working in schools when I was fourteen. I described how I'd worked my way through all the various positions schools have on my way to becoming an administrator including, bus driver. I told them, even though I knew from experience it wouldn't exactly endear them to me.

I found on previous interviews that my rags-to-not-so-rich-riches story was disliked by rich people. I could tell you that they hate people who earn their position rather than inherit it but I think it was mostly that my plebian background screamed poor person. It was the very thing the people at Sunnydale liked about me, bless their misdemeanor laden hearts.

Still, the panel was all wide smiles with more straight, blindingly white teeth than a month of toothpaste ads. I didn't mention why I was presently unemployed and looking for a job.

The woman on the end already decided

she didn't like me. I could read her mind. She couldn't say why if you asked her but the decision was there just the same.

I wore my black pinstripe suit with a light pastel blue silk tie and matching silk hanky. I'd lost weight and felt like I was swimming in it. That and Mrs. Mean-face's decision to not like me was eroding my self confidence fast.

There was a pause when I finished the, "a little about yourself," portion of the interview. They were shuffling papers, sliding the last report from the last interview under the little stack of papers each had in front of them in preparation for the questions portion of the interview. The superintendent seemed to feel his role as M.C. required that he be sure somebody was talking at all times said, "I see you worked at Sunnydale. Whew! They had some troubles there!"

His comment along with his just-folks talking style and his shit-eating smile detonated an explosion of anger in my head. To my credit, at that moment, I did nothing to indicate the consuming rage I was experiencing.

I smiled slowly and said, "It's a good school, they just got some bad publicity."

He nodded graciously, his smile downgraded to a grin.

I said, "But ya know what I think . . ." Then I did the absolute dumbest thing I could ever do: I told them what I thought.

When it was over I shook their hands, stopped off at the men's room on the way out to wash my hands, then left. Surprisingly, I didn't spend the whole two hour drive home berating myself for my stupidity. I was all out of anger. Instead, my thoughts drifted back to my first few weeks on the job at Sunnydale.

It was amazing how much of my time was spent with student discipline and it seemed that all the students who misbehaved all wound up the same place-my office. The only thing more plentiful than their misbehaviors was their excuses. I wasn't at Sunnydale a long time before I had heard them all.

"I was holding those cigarettes for some friends, they ain't mine."

"I swear to you Mr. Farmer, I was not cheating on da test. I only had da book open because I was checking to see if da teacher asked the right question!"

"I forgot that firecracker was in my pants cause my mom forgot to wash them, then the other kids dared me to set if off."

They never seemed to stop coming and a big reason for that was the teachers themselves. They would shave five to ten minutes off both ends of class. And in all those wasted moments the students would, get into disputes that metamorphosed into fights, steal, run around the classroom, throw things out the window, set off fireworks, destroy property, and about a hundred other things anyone who knows anything about human adolescents could have predicted.

The teachers would hide in their rooms during class changes instead of stand in the hallway. Needless to say the students, ever mindful of the attention of the machine, would exploit that lapse to illicit ends. The unsupervised hall moments led to running, throwing objects, groping and of course, fighting.

The best way to deal with school discipline is to avoid having to deal with it in the first place. And as corny as it sounds, nothing prevents misbehavior better than a good lesson plan. If a teacher keeps students busy and can generate interest in the subject matter, most students won't want to misbehave.

The teachers at Sunnydale wouldn't waste their time developing lessons that were even remotely interesting. The funny thing is, if I turned in such a bad performance on teacher in-service day when it was their turn to be students, they would scream their objections to Czar Superintendent Mayonnaise. Teachers are the worst students.

I began to develop a theory about the teachers at Sunnydale. I postulated, in my mind only, that something in their environment caused damage to the portion of the brain that controls judgment. It was the only way I could explain their shocking stupidity in their relations with students. I had to deal with the fallout from their lack of discretion every day.

The cycle would begin with a bored student breaking a relatively minor school rule. The teacher would overreact and then do or say something incredibly stupid or offensive. The escalation would begin and I would be called in to remove the student.

In one instance I had a young Social Studies teacher begin to berate a student in the hallway in front of his peers. The teacher, who was tall and rather muscular, stepped forward as he began to yell. The student stepped back. The teacher, still ranting his rage, took another step forward. The student stepped back. This chain of behaviors repeated and resulted in the student literally being backed into a corner. The confrontation ended with the student throwing a balled up piece of paper in the teacher's face and running off.

Now the problem became my problem. I can't overlook a student deliberately throwing something in a teacher's face but I can't punish the kid because the teacher is an asshole. I have to be Solomon the Wise and solve the issue in a mature way even though the whole time I want to kick the teacher in the ass for being such a fucking idiot.

The sad irony of the whole mess was that in the end, my solution relied heavily on the maturity of the student in question. He acknowledged his responsibility in the matter and accepted the consequences. In a perfect world the teacher would have been at least as adult as the student. But it isn't a perfect world and I was in Sunnydale so I had to ask the teacher nicely to not belittle any students in front of their peers and then physically intimidate them and to please, no matter what, don't back them into a corner. Thank you.

I would say that ninety percent of the discipline problems I encountered at Sunnydale were a result of one or more of the adults screwing up somehow and as bothersome as that was, the worst was that other ten percent. A small cadre of students, as with every school I was ever involved with, were real criminals. The criminal element at Sunnydale was hardcore.

That's why I immediately set out to determine if my tip that a student named Matt Dissento had a knife was accurate, and that he actually had the knife on him. I wasn't happy about the possibility of having to deknifeify a student but I sure as hell couldn't let him stab someone.

I was making my way down the main hallway when I encountered Stubby at the cross hall. He was on patrol. I figured I'd bring him with me on this. Very often students will attempt to evade punishment by redirecting the focus from their misdeeds to a discussion of how the administrator did not do his job right.

Given that this tactic was classic misdirection I termed it Abra Cadabra. I knew that in an instance of such magnitude where the punishment was high, a second party witness would not necessarily prevent a student from pulling an Abra Cadabra but it would help shorten the argument. Plus, Stubby could give an accurate description to the cops if the kid did decide to stab my guts out rather than talk it out.

"Ay, Mr. Stub-bee-owitz, why don't you walk with me?"

"Whatsup?"

"I got a tip from one of my snitches that a student has a knife on him."

"Yeah, I got it," he said, and fell into step with me.

We both proceeded down the hall to the classroom Mat was supposed to be in. I motioned to Stubby to wait outside while I got the kid. I always took matters outside the classroom. Students are less likely to posture if there is no one there to enjoy the show. And in this case, if the kid did have a weapon, I wanted him away from the other students.

I stepped into the room and waited for the teacher to acknowledge my presence. This was Mr. Hadley's class. He was a Science teacher who could barely manage a classroom yet managed to get the local paper to write articles about what a great teacher he was at least once a month. He was a short goof in his mid fifties whose excess weight all settled around his mid section, making him look as if he'd swallowed a flying saucer.

"Hello Mr. Hadley, can I speak with Matt Dissento please."

Mr. Hadley nodded toward Matt who was sitting towards the back of the room with a small pile of books on his desk and his coat on the back of his chair. He had a look of surprise. Then an expression of wonderment as to why the assistant principal, any assistant principal, would want to speak with him, adorned his face as he got up. I had to hand it to him, it was a polished act.

He got up from his desk then walked toward the door leaving his oversized coat hanging on the back of the chair. I stepped out the door after him.

"Matt, what's all this crazy talk about you having a knife on you?" I asked, as soon as I was sure the door to the classroom had completely closed. I was hoping my directness would catch him without a plausible denial.

"What?"

He's stalling. Not a good sign.

"Did you bring a knife to school?"

"No, you can check me if you want."

That was too quick and too willing.

"Well, things being what they are, I am going to have to check. You're saying you don't have a knife on you or in your locker?"

It's a good bet the kid didn't have the knife on him but he could be trying to bluff me in the hope that his willingness to be searched would suffice and I wouldn't then actually search him. I added the locker to see if anything registered on his face. Regardless of his Oscar-winning performance I was going to check both. I had to, just to be safe.

"No," he said with an air of innocence that bordered on overplaying his hand.

"Matt I'm going to have to search you, and then I'm going to check your locker. You understand?"

I figured now that he knows that he and his locker are going to get searched he might come clean.

"Thas cool, you do what you gotta do," he said in a way that conveyed he sympathized with my situation and my searching him and his locker was perfectly understandable.

Before I could even take a step towards him to do the search, Stubby stepped over and frisked Matt with lighting speed and precision. The kid definitely didn't have the knife on him.

I knew this kid brought a knife to school. I felt it. I tried to shake him but he didn't even wobble when I mentioned searching the locker so the knife isn't there and my associate Stubby gave him a frisk job that would put a Turkish customs official to shame, so it's a good bet he has the knife somewhere else. But I know something he doesn't know that I know.

"Matt, I'm going to ask you one more time. Did you bring a knife to school?" I asked gently.

That last one was the set up so that later when the arguments started about who did what I could say he denied having the knife several times. The tag line will be, 'He knowingly lied to me even though I gave him several opportunities to tell the truth.'

"I already told you, no," he said, becoming indignant.

I kept my eyes locked on Matt's face and said, "Mr. Stubby, could you please go in the classroom and get Mr. Dissento's coat. Thank you."

"Yeah sure," Stubby said and stepped into the classroom.

Matt's confidence and growing indignation disappeared instantly and he began to look nervous. I watched as the apprehension spread across his face like one of those speeded up science films where a flower blooms rapidly.

"I'm not going to lie to you Mr. Farmer. I do have a knife in my coat," he said with a note of panic in his voice. It was an amazing transition given its distance over such a short period of time.

"Well actually, if that is the case, you did lie to me," I said flatly.

"No, Mr. Farmer, I just remembered that I had that knife in my coat."

Just then Stubby came out of the classroom with the coat in his hands. He started going through the gangster wrap and quickly located the knife. It was a folding knife with a five inch blade. He handed it to me.

The sight of me slipping that gleaming weapon into my suit coat pocket must have struck a nerve in Matt because he started talking faster.

"Mr. Farmer, I swear I forgot that knife was in my coat because it's not really my knife."

"It's not yours?"

"No."

"Then whose knife is it?"

"Uh . . . It's nobody's. I found it."

"Where did you find it?"

"I found it on the way to school. I was going to turn it in to you but I forgot about it. I . . . saw the knife then I thought someone could get hurt with it so I picked it up and put it in my pocket."

"So you were really just acting in the public interest when you brought that knife to school?"

"Thas right . . . What?"

"Well, I tell you what, let's you and I head down to my office and take care of this matter. Mr. Stubby will get your books for you. Let's go."

Chapter 8

I entered the Principal's office and sat down. Apple was sitting behind his desk, leaning back in his chair, staring at the computer screen. He had his clasped hands resting on his big belly.

"You called Sahib?"

He paused before responding. He waited the exact amount of time necessary to confirm that he was an ass of titanic proportions then said, "This paper-work is too much. I feel locked in my office."

"It's killer," I said, thinking, who the hell is this guy kidding? Rick did all his paperwork for him.

"Did Rick show you how to set the calendar on CompuSchool?"

"Aye he did."

"Good. I want you to make sure that it is kept up-to-date."

"Got it," I said, knowing what he'd just said was a precursor to what he really wanted to tell me. Years of being a school administrator had rendered him incapable of being direct. It was like living on the moon so long that when you came back to earth you couldn't stand up.

"I also want you to go through the teachers' schedules and get someone who is free to cover in-school suspension for fifth period."

Ah, so here it is. "What's wrong with Mr. Stueben? He's been covering ISS that period," I said.

Mr. Stueben was a drunken reject from the Steel Industry. Once upon a time the town of Sunnydale was flush with people and money. As the fortunes of the steel industry declined, so did everything about Sunnydale. Like piranhas trapped in a pool of water after the floods receded, they turned on each other as the food supply in their little pool dwindled.

Sunnydale still had a steel industry but it was a fraction of its former size. The demand for quality in their workers grew as the pool of applicants desperate for work grew. Stueben, the drunken ass, just didn't make the grade.

Stueben did have one qualification, however, that made him a valuable hire for Sunnydale, he had a brother on the school board. But even with those perfect credentials and the lax quality control standards of Sunnydale, the best they could fit Stueben, the idiot, in the organization was to make him Athletic Director/Driver Ed. Teacher. A position which required so little brain power to do a drunken chimp could have served nicely. And I probably would have preferred that alternative to Stueben.

It's true that most school district hierarchies are ga ga over sports and schools routinely devote an enormous quantity of their resources to their sports program. And even though I was never a coach, a rarity among administrators, I wasn't opposed to sports itself.

My criticism of the sports programs in schools is that they are not in line with the mission of the school. The purpose of any school is to increase learning. The sports program in any school should serve that function. Schools never exploit the advantage sports give them in that area. It's a matter of not enough bang for the buck.

When I was an Alternative Education Teacher I used to play basketball with the students after school three days a week. Alternative Education is where they send the "At-Risk" students, the kids generally disliked by the establishment because they are short on compliance and long on needs. The kind of kids who would much rather play basketball with their teacher after school than go back to their shitty homes.

Most Alt. Ed. Students had the mentality of prisoners of war. To them, school was a place you went for six hours a day and someone poked you with a stick the entire time. But during the basketball games they were interested, and while we played they generally relented on their duty to provide resistance to the enemy. I would do nearly as much teaching during our games as when I had them hostage in class.

Alas, most sports programs are populated by idiots who are there because they truly believe there is some significance to the games themselves. They could never understand that it doesn't matter who wins the Homecoming game. It's all shit. The point is to use the moment of victory, or loss, as a teachable moment. To teach the value of hard work, sportsmanship, and so on. To put it in terms the loyal members of the jockocracy would understand: every maneuver within the sports program should be to move the ball down the field; the ball being, of course, learning.

"He made a deal with the Superintendent," Apple said, looking back to his computer, hoping to imply that he had better things, more important things to do than discuss the issue with me. Like most leaders who are a few quarts low on leadership, he saw any discussion about decisions as insurgent. "He will be coming in later in the morning because as Athletic Director he will be covering the games,"

"Wasn't he Athletic Director last year?"

"Yes," he said, still eyeing the computer.

"What has changed?"

He turned towards me and just smiled slowly.

"Oh, I get it. . . He has a brother on the

school board."

He nodded slowly. Ordinarily, Apple wasn't shy when it came to words. He was just ensuring plausible deniability by not verbalizing anything to me while communicating the whole bit.

"We don't have enough guys to cover all the classes we have now. Not to mention, how do I explain to the teachers that the guy who only teaches two classes a day needs more time off?"

As Athletic Director, Stueben was only scheduled to teach two Driver Ed. Classes and one period monitoring the in-school suspension room while the teacher there went to lunch. This absurdly light schedule was in deference to his alleged athletic director responsibilities.

Apple just shrugged and said, "I don't know. All I know is that, I do what I'm told. The Superintendent said to get someone to cover for Mr. Stueben so I will."

"So you're saying we won't have to cover the games?" I asked, looking for a good side to all this because his last statement told me it was a done deal.

"Oh no, one of us will have to be there. Stueben isn't capable of covering the games himself."

"So some teacher is going to have to work extra because Stueben has a brother on the school board. I guess it's better to know people than things."

"How's your friend Lou?"

This was probably the real, real reason for our meeting. The other stuff he could have easily emailed.

"We had a frank discussion," I said, smiling slightly.

"About what?"

"I am not entirely sure, but our

conversation did remind me to get my booster shots."

"He's nuts," he declared.

Apple said that about everyone. In fact, he said it with such frequency that I am sure he said it about me. The more I worked at Sunnydale the less inclined I was to argue the point however.

"I agree. Hey, did you get that T.A.P. team training request I sent?"

The Teacher Assistance Program, aka T.A.P., was a program started to identify students who may be having drug problems, sexual abuse, etc. and get them the help they needed. Originally it was a good plan but like so many school programs, as soon as it started working, threats of lawsuits surfaced so the powers that be pulled the teeth out of it. Once it was rendered ineffectual all complaints about it ceased.

My interest in it was purely bureaucratic.

I had to take the three-day training course given by the state Department of Education so that I could administer the program. I needed my ticket punched.

"Yes, I looked into it but the training was canceled. Not enough people signed up," he said.

"Wow, I wouldn't have expected that."

"Yeah. What's the story with Woods?"

Our conversations often skipped from subject to subject. It was a shorthand form of conversation designed to get in the maximum amount of information before the inevitable interruption.

"You mean other than the fact that he has been a teacher for sixteen years and still can't read a schedule or control a class?"

"Yeah," he laughed. "We got testing next week. Are we ready for it?"

"Yes. I gave each of the teachers their

marching orders, I've arranged to have extra calculators on hand and each of the students has been issued a suicide pill. We are totally ready."

"We'd better be," he said.

Testing is everything in schools because most states link funding to the results. Better scores, more bucks. The ironic thing about standardized testing is that nearly all the state governments manipulate the process so that the results look better than they really are. Or, to put it another way, the guys who make the tests cheat. The system has become so adept at being dishonest with itself there is almost no way to determine where the bullshit begins and where it ends.

"Oh I know," I said. "I spoke with Dr. Mayonnaise the other day and he promised to personally kick me in the balls if anything goes wrong."

"He'll do worse than that, believe me.

What's the story with the kid with the knife?"

"Not much, he admitted to bringing it to school. I called his mom and his probation officer, suspended him and did all the usual paper work. We're going to have to set up the board review of the case since it was a weapons violation."

"Yeah, I'll set that up," he said leaning over to write a note on a scratch pad.

"Ya know,"

I paused for a minute to organize what I was about to say which caused Apple to look up. Now the moment was more dramatic than I intended but I saw no reason I should not continue.

"While I was checking out this whole knife thing, there was a moment when I was going to frisk the kid and Stubby stepped forward and frisked the kid. Which wasn't wrong, it's just . . . I don't know . . .He frisked the kid like a real pro. Like he had done that sort of thing before . . .many times."

"Well . . ." He was about to say something. He caught himself in the nick of time.

"What? You know something?"

He smiled broadly, "I just do what I'm told. I was told to make him a hall monitor and that's what I did. Speaking of which, the Superintendent called me this morning. He wants you to be in his office this afternoon for your evaluation."

What the hell was that, I wondered after I left his office. He was trying to tell me something without telling me. I thought about that conversation all the way to the Praetor's office that afternoon.

Dr. Mayonnaise's office looked as if the decorator was not sure if he was decorating an office or a frat house. It was a curious mélange of sports memorabilia and office furnishings. It had a blue rug and brown varnished woodwork. Still, it is likely one would overlook all that to stare at the monstrosity that was his chair. It was a wing back so ridiculously overstuffed and oversized it made the aircraft carrier sized desk in front of it look small.

When I got there His Lordship had my evaluation on the desk. It was weird that he would be evaluating me since we had almost no contact most of the time. Whatever he knew about me at work he'd heard from other people. I was just hoping he talked to the ones that liked me and not the ones who didn't.

He went through it with me and was quite generous with his praise but still it had the feel of make believe. I mean, who would object to being called the world's greatest lover, even if one wasn't really sure the honor was deserved? He said nice things about me; I wasn't going to argue.

"So do you have any questions before I sign your evaluation?" he asked, holding a pen in his right hand. He was holding it over the paper like he was waiting for the starter gun to go off.

"No, I'm happy you like my work," I said. After a moment's hesitation, I added, "Well there is one thing that did come up."

"What?" The pen hand moved ever so slightly back away from the paper.

I plunged in. "I was wondering about Stubby."

"The hall monitor?"

"Yeah, I was wondering what the story was with his background. What's his work history?"

"All our employees get a background check before they are hired. If anyone asks just tell them that."

His voice changed slightly and the pen went all the way back to his side. I decided to proceed with caution but to proceed nevertheless.

"I'm asking. I have certain reservations about him."

"Well you keep them to yourself. His background isn't your area. You're an assistant principal who is about to get a good first evaluation. Let it go."

His voice took a totally different tone. I had never seen him this close to losing his cool. The pen hand even twitched a little. Not a good sign, I thought. I was so surprised by this I stupidly asked, "Let it go?"

What the hell was "it," anyway? Sounds like I hit a nerve.

"Yeah," he said, gaining a little composure.

We stared at each other for a moment. I

nodded to let him know I got the message, even though I really didn't. I understood the "let it go" part but I didn't get the "why" of it. I really wasn't sure if my question was legitimate or if I was reverting to my old habit of asking too many questions.

Mayonnaise smiled slightly. I could see he was satisfied he won the dick length contest. He brought the pen down on a damn fine evaluation, I had mostly earned. I had worked hard and I must confess in that moment my thoughts turned to self-congratulations.

Mayonnaise got up out of his colossal chair, walked around the oversized desk and handed me the evaluation. I turned to walk out and he put his arm around me and walked me to the door. His gesture was obvious and it brought my thoughts back to the subject of Stubby.

"Look, Harris, you're going to be in this business a long time. You need to know that in order to get along, you've got to go along. You're doing a fine job. Keep it up but forget about this issue. It's handled."

"Okay, sure, I know. I just do what I'm told," I wanted to get his arm off me and the hell out of there. Dr. Charm was giving me the creeps something awful. There was no way I was not going to look into it now.

"Right," he said putting out his hand, the one that just signed my evaluation. I shook it like a dumbass.

I said, "Thanks," and walked out.

Chapter 9

She was talking to me, possibly at me. I don't know. I wasn't anywhere near paying attention. She was probably talking about money or jobs. She did that a lot lately. If you were there you would swear I was internalizing it like Vygotsky would have loved.

I had perfected the art of listening while at Sunnydale. I acquired the bulk of my skills from Apple. He got it from the principal before him, Ron Something. Ron, it was said, not only soaked up complaints like Superman's towel soaks up water but he took notes while doing it.

No one who left his office, whatever their grievances, left feeling that they hadn't been heard. Just as surely as Mr. Something made them feel their worries were being attended to, he disposed of his notes about ten seconds after they left and promptly forgot the entire conversation.

It's true that in this instance I didn't have a note pad out but I had Apple and old Ron both beat. I was disposing of everything my wife was saying without ever even letting it in. She was oblivious and so was I. And, as proud as I was of my ability to bypass the conversation, I was a bit apprehensive because I knew that leaving my mind with nothing to do was risky. Just then, the phone rang.

"Harris Farmer Assistant Principal, Catcher in the Rye. How may I help you?" I heard myself answer. Myself from a long time ago.

"Mr. Farmer I be missing two tests. You didn't give them back to me so I can't give them to the students. You better find them," Mrs. Nickels said.

"Are you sure I lost them?"

"Sure I'm sure," she said angrily. "I didn't be losin no tests. You be responsible for them tests. I left them in yo office with da rest. You better be finding them tests!"

"I'm on it," I said and shot out of my chair. I'm not even sure if I put the phone back in its carriage.

Losing two tests is a big deal. All standardized tests have to be given in a standardized way and if they are not, the state can zero out the entire school's scores. That is not something I would want to have to report to Mayonnaise who surely would have had me break the bad news to the board.

I started to think about all the places the two tests could have wound up and calculated the most likely scenario. My testing plan called for all the teachers to bring the tests to my office at the end of each day so it was possible that one of the other teachers picked up the two tests while grabbing their stack of tests in the morning. It was also possible that the two slid off the top of

Ms. Nickels' stack to the one adjacent. I checked the two teachers who had their tests next to Ms. Nickels'. Then I went to the teacher who was most likely to do something stupid.

After checking on Mr. Woods and discovering he did not have them, I headed over to the library to check with the guidance counselor proctoring the miscellaneous students that always crop up when giving a test.

The guidance counselor assigned to me was a tall, thin narcissist who never had the same hairdo two days in a row. If she spent any time not goofing off I never saw it. I had discussed the matter of her incompetence with Apple a few times but for reasons I was never able to determine, she was an untouchable.

But I wasn't going to see her. I was going to see Mrs. Honey. It's true that the only thing more useless than a guidance counselor, is two guidance counselors. And I've said it myself more than a few times. However, Mrs. Honey, in homage to the enigmatic nature of Sunnydale, was the best guidance counselor that ever lived. She worked hard and was damned effective. I never encountered a guidance counselor with so much oomph. Every time I was around her I wanted to wrestle her to the ground and extract some of her DNA for cloning.

I thought maybe Mrs. Honey could shed some light on the subject. She was unable to help. She just shook her head slowly. I could see from her expression she understood, as perhaps no other non administrator in the school could, just how much trouble I was in.

I ran out of logical explanations for the missing tests, which really got the old adrenaline flowing. I could feel heat and humiliation radiating from my face. Sweat poured out of me and I started to feel panic rising. I'd worked through all the likely possibilities. Even though my mind desperately wanted to slip away to a comfortable place, I forced myself to consider the unlikely possibilities. Then it hit me, it was both the most likely and least likely.

I headed up to Miss Nickels' class. When I got there I saw all but two of her students were working on their tests. Miss Nickels was at her desk with the two students whose tests were missing. They were hovering at the corner of her desk to her left.

"Hello Miss Nickels."

"Mr. Farmer did you find them tests?" she nearly shouted. "You never gave them back to me. Y'all are responsible for them tests ya know."

She was letting me know that she was not to blame for this mistake. It was not a shot across the bow, it was a pre-emptive strike. Even though I joked with Miss Nickels and liked what I knew of her, I was not surprised she would turn on me so abruptly. After all, I knew she was a teacher when I started liking her.

I walked over to her while she was ranting at me. I stood just to her right.

"I didn't find them yet but I think I will find them real soon."

I looked down and reached to the stack of papers on the front right corner of her desk. Right on top of the stack of papers were the two tests. I picked them up and handed them to her.

"Are these the tests?"

Her eyes grew wide. She sputtered then laughed.

"Yes, they be the tests," she said with a wide smile, shaking her head. "I is sorry to put you through all that! Yes. I is sorry."

"No problem Ms. Nickels," I said. Then I said, *'fucking idiot,'* to myself.

Chapter 10

I was in my second month as an administrator before I went to my first board meeting at Sunnydale. All the administrators were required to go. There was absolutely no earthly reason for this except the Superintendent wanted us there so that if a question of blame came up, he could direct the complainer directly at one of us.

Sunnydale's school board had many complaints. They would listen to anybody about anything and then bring it up in front of the public like it was Gospel truth. It was incredibly annoying to have to sit in the back of the room and listen to them complain about us concerning matters that never happened. And is if that weren't enough, we would have to answer to whatever complaints their specious logic could dream up.

The school board is the ultimate power in a school district. Technically, they run the district via the use of the chief executive, the superintendent. They set the policy and we who are about to die, carry it out.

Sunnydale's board was very much like nearly every school board in America. That is, none of them ever taught so much as a single class at any grade level. They were woefully ignorant of the educational process and, like many school board members I have known, not interested in finding out. To combat this phenomenon, many states have required new school board members to take a course before assuming their duties, but our state hadn't gotten around to it.

Oh yeah, Sunnydale's board had one other distinction: they were all morons. None of them had college degrees and they all had a chip on their shoulders about it. I sometimes wondered if they got a special thrill out of ordering around guys in suits with college degrees. It would explain why they were so abusive to us.

The room ordinarily used for board meetings was not overly large and it was right across the hall from the superintendent's secret exit. He had it installed after an angry parent caught up with him as he was leaving one day. It was complete with a peep hole.

The room was not very large and it was dominated by five fold-out tables arranged in a u-shape. There were about twelve chairs at the open end, should anyone decide to show up. Mostly they didn't. There were several chairs located in the back corner behind the closed end of the shoe for the administrators. The Superintendent sat at the apex and the Assistant Superintendent, Ray Dirt, sat to Mayonnaise's left.

Ray was a member of the jockocracy in good standing. He was an ex-coach who could barely read and write, but he was true to his prime directive, which was to make sure that nothing, education included, impeded the sports program. He was the only member of the school administration who was never publicly criticized by the board.

Apple, whose football team went up against Ray's once upon a time, told me that Ray was a good coach but somewhat dull in the tactics department. He also said that when Ray was younger he could run like a deer. I'd say he'd thickened quite a bit since then.

The board was composed of five white males, all in their 40'and 50's, two black women in their 40's, one young white woman and Mustard, the only black male. Judging by their respective sizes I would say that unless the laws of physics were severely changed, none of them could run like a deer and their wardrobe could be aptly described as a plebian paean to polyester.

The Board Secretary was a large black woman in her mid forties. She was Biffy's mother and she was having an affair with Lou. That bit of knowledge both horrified and mesmerized me at the same time. I couldn't imagine how two people of such size could make love. And how is it that I, who never interacted with them outside of work, would know they were involved in an affair and their spouses not know? It was all so sordid, blubbery and gross.

Lou smacked the gavel and the buzz in the room stopped. Everyone stood and recited the pledge to the flag.

I worked in a rural district once wherein they recited a prayer before every board meeting. It was creepy and wildly unethical but I sure as hell wasn't going to argue with them about it. Religious people scare me.

"Let's all come to order," Lou's smooth vellum voice oozed. He could have been a DJ for a Jazz station. "First order of business is to read the minutes from the Board's last meeting," he said.

Just then, Mr. Stueben, brother of the Athletic Director, said, "I propose we waive the reading of the minutes."

They all voted for that no problem. Sunnydale's board was not real interested in the proprieties. They had little tolerance for niceties and absolutely no understanding of Robert's Rules of Order. Discussions frequently became argument replete with yelling and cursing.

Mr. Goldwater was the board's gadfly. Every class has a kid like him, short on patience, in love with the sound of his own voice and desperate for attention, be it good or bad.

He looked as if he were hiding a wine barrel under his 1970's vintage suit. His face looked like a cartoon version of a real face. His eyes were little slits and his nose was short and sort of pig snoutish. He had a slight lisp which tended to make every crazy thing he said seem even crazier.

"I just have a few things, the first is: Why did we cancel the Halloween Day parade at the Elementary?" Goldwater asked.

"That is a good question," Lou said with an accusatory tone, swinging his head towards the principal of the Elementary School.

Goldwater went on as if he hadn't heard, "It seems to me the kids were happy with it and the community enjoyed seeing them dress up in all their costumes. So why did we cancel it? Uh, it seems to me if we are doing something that works we should keep it up, not cancel it."

"I don't know," Lou said.

Ned Piper was the principal of the elementary school. Sunnydale only had two schools. The elementary was built in the late 19th century. It was a four story brick building and even though its designers really built the hell out of it, and even though it received meticulous care, its days were numbered. It served about six hundred students.

Ned was a short muscular man in his late fifties, every bit the Marine he was nearly forty years before when he was sent to Vietnam. He was a disciplined man who was never far from some form of the Globe and Anchor symbol of the Marine Corps. On this night, it was on his tie.

Ned was hard working, decent and had the unfortunate habit of believing in a code of honor. The Board's public humiliation of us once every month really offended him. He understandably didn't like to have his decisions questioned like this. Who could blame him for that?

After Goldwater finished his soliloquy, Lou swung his head to the Superintendent as if to say, 'Well how about it, dumbass?' Then the Superintendent swung his head towards Ned as if to say, 'You made the decision, now defend it. You won't get any help from me. I'm a scumbag whose philosophy of leadership is every man for himself and God for us all.'

Ned got pissed. I could see a vein in his neck start to pulse. No doubt he was wishing he could call in artillery on this group of pricks.

"The Halloween parade was canceled because it was a waste of time. I couldn't justify it while our test scores have been so low-" Ned started to explain when Goldwater starts talking as if Ned hadn't said anything.

"From what I understand the other districts have their parades. It seems to me the kids might need a break."

The Reverend Beach chimed in, "I agree. I can't see why we cancelled it. I apologize if I'm talking out of turn here, but why don't we have the parade?"

The Reverend was always apologizing when he spoke. It was damned annoying. He always wore golf clothes. It was his favorite pastime. In fact, according to Rick Bird, the good Reverend became a man of the cloth because it was the one profession next to actually being a professional golfer, something he was far from being, he calculated would afford him the most time to golf.

Judging from the bulge pulsing in Ned's neck I would say he was angrier now than before. It looked like one of those South American Bull Frogs. He said, "It was my decision to make as Principal and it was the right decision. Any time you want my resignation you can have it!"

Ned got up and stalked out of the room. Apple, Rick and I exchanged genuine looks of surprise. None of us thought he was going to do that. That was an 'I dare you' to a bunch of idiots who could only respond by taking the dare. Ned was finished, that much was clear.

I only met Ned a few times but he seemed like a decent, hard-working man who always put the interests of his students first. However, he was forgetting two essential facts about schools: To the mindset of school personnel, appearing as if one is doing one's job is the same thing as *actually* doing one's job. That Halloween parade made it look like the school was doing its job even if it was just a bunch of kids walking around in costumes. And, as I said before, if the school board thinks you are doing a good job or thinks you are doing a bad job, *you are*.

But here's the most shocking part. The whole room erupted into conversations a beat after Ned left.

That's when I heard Lou say to his cetacean sized secretary, "That's okay we'll get the rest of them later."

Get the rest of them later? Just what the hell did he mean by that? I am guessing he meant Rick, Apple and me. I didn't like the sound of it.

I turned to Apple, "Did you hear that?"

He just nodded slightly, not the least bit surprised by it.

After the Ned Piper show, the board went into Executive Session. Executive Session is a nonpublic meeting of the board, where even we, the administrators, were asked to go out and wait in the hall, which we did.

While I was out in the hall I ran into Ms. Elvina Denton. She was a small black woman who survived so much harshness in her early years I surmised she was probably the toughest person in the universe. She was short, slightly hunched and rail thin.

I first met her on the first day of school. I had arrived before everyone. The sun was just coming up over the horizon, splashing yellow light everywhere when I pulled into the empty lot. The place was positively deserted and the only sound was my heels hitting the pavement as I walked toward the main entrance.

I always park away from all other cars. It never hurts to walk a little and I don't trust other drivers with my paint job. At Sunnydale I always parked in the far corner in clear view of the District Office. With that collection of nosy old Biddys watching the lot, my car had less chance of being touched than an algebra text in the school library.

As I said, there was no movement and no sound other than my shoes so I was a bit startled when I saw Elvina standing near one of the pillars that held up the concrete portico at the main entrance.

As soon as our eyes locked she said, "Good Morning," in a soft southern accent I pegged as being from one of the Carolinas.

"Hello," I said and smiled.

"Do y'all work here?"

"I do today. Harris Farmer, newly minted assistant principal. It's a pleasure to meet you. But I gotta tell you, you're awfully early. School doesn't start for quite some time. Still, it does this old heart good to see a student so anxious for school on the first day."

She shook my hand. Her hand was bony and delicate with onion paper-thin skin. I got the sense that this is what it would be like to shake hands with a bird, if birds had hands.

"How'd you do? I am Elvina Denton. It's nice to meet y'all. I'm not a student here."

"Oh."

"I had heard they hired a new principal. Are you married? Do you have any children?"

"One wife, several children."

"Ohhh. Well I'm sure you have a lovely wife."

"She's okay. But then I figure with my movie star looks and rebel ways I was bound to get a quality wife. When you think about it, she should consider herself lucky she made the cut."

"You joke young man but a wife be very impotant fo a man."

"Perhaps, but I don't think you were waiting out here in the chilly morning air just to discuss my marriage."

"I'm here to get tickets for the football game."

"Football eh? Well apparently I'm the only one here and I don't know where the tickets are. I don't think I can help you but why don't you step inside with me and wait in the office away from this morning chill?"

"Thank you, young man. I just know you'll do well here."

Elvina had a self possession that only people born before the advent of the television could have and even though the old lady was from another dimension, I liked her. And as before, I hadn't noticed her standing outside the board room till I nearly stepped on her. I swear the lady was part ninja.

"Ay Mrs. Denton, how you doing?"

"Jes fine young man. How you be doin?"

"Okay today I suppose."

"I hear you been workin a lotta hours."

"It's not just a job, it's a way of life."

I had been working a lot of hours.

"I know you be funnin with me but you ain't gonna be no good to yo family if all you be doin is workin."

"That is true," I said, because it was.

"You got ta take some time for yourself and yo family."

"Yes ma'am," I said.

We chatted a little more about several of her grandchildren, she seemed to have about a thousand of them. Then the meeting was called back to order and I can't relate what happened after that point because I was so busy thinking about what had happened with Ned.

That whole night turned out to be very disturbing. Yet, as soon as I left the parking lot my thoughts turned to my family. It seems old lady Elvina really got inside my head.

I spent my drive home thinking about my wife and children and my thoughts drifted to the night I met my wife, which is something I hadn't thought about in a long time. I'd been married so happily for so long, it seemed like I had always been married, like there was never a time before my wife.

But, of course there was a time before. We first met in a bar and, improbably, given her good looks and my Elephant Man looks, I, for lack of a better expression, picked her up.

It was the sort of bar adults frequent. I doubt there was anybody in the place below the age of thirty five besides us and her friends. It had a blonde wood floor with a rough hewn wooden post and rail fence that divided the booths and small dance area from the bar area which ran the length of the wall. I might have mistaken it for a country western bar but for the dress of the patrons, the rock music coming from the jukebox and the paraphernalia hanging from the walls and ceiling, arranged there to give the place an Ivy League feel.

I was standing alone on the edge of the empty dance floor near the jukebox swaying slightly. I had my eyes closed. The music and the beer were mixing in my head in just the right amount. I was very nearly drunk and working on it assiduously when it occurred to me that if people had gills, nobody would ever drown again and I should start working on a way to install gills on people.

The more I thought about it the more I liked the idea. But then my thoughts turned to marriage because water, gills on humans and marriage are very much related when one's intellect is operating in the upper register of blood alcohol level.

Most of my friends had married off long ago. Lots of people got married. I reasoned I could do it too if I could just find some woman stupid enough to hitch her future with mine. The trick, I mused, is to get her to the altar before she gets to know me.

I wouldn't say I had an epiphany, exactly. But there was something of a revelation, a turning of the corner if you will, in the realization I should find someone to share my life with. Naturally, I would want to see if all this still made sense when I sobered up, but now was not the time to be sober so I opened my eyes to seek out another brew. When I did, I noticed the tall busty brunette leaning against the corner of the jukebox opposite the corner I was occupying.

I hadn't seen her there, and then there she was. Then one thought tumbled into another and I reasoned that maybe it was a sign I should go talk to her. Perhaps our conversation could lead to positive results. At the very least, I could get some feedback on the gills for people idea. I stepped over to her.

She had jaw dropping looks. Her mid length hair had just enough body to curl around her angular face. Her nose was the perfect length and her almost black eyes sparkled in the half lit bar.

"You look bored," I said.

"I came here with some friends but they seemed to have left me," she said, looking around, scanning the crowd for the missing friends.

"I'm sure they are around here somewhere. Did your friends drive you here?" I said, as if I just wanted to help her and my attention had nothing to do with her class 'A' knockers.

"Well I came here with my friend Doris."

"My name is Harris," I said, not because I didn't hear her remark about Doris, but because when she glanced at me after searching the bar with her eyes I had an insane desire for her to know my name.

"My name is Dairy."

"What?"

"Dairy"

"Oh! I'll bet there is a story behind that name."

"Yeah"

Not good. I was moving in too fast. Of course there was a story to go with the name! A story told a million times to friends and beaus at the dinner table, not some guy she just met in a bar with saws, canoes and shit hanging from the ceiling. *Dope!*

"What's your last name?" I asked, risking her wondering if I was a stalker.

"Dell"

"What?"

"Dell"

Her name was Dairy Dell? I would have thought a bunch of real funny things at that point. Things I most probably never would have said aloud anyway. But the beer, the boobs and the banter was using up so much RAM that I just thought, "Huh?" Not a great moment for me.

"Dairy Dell, that's a name you don't hear every day."

"Actually, I do," she said.

It was quick, clever and she said it dryly, almost matter-of-factly. I liked that. She didn't consider such wit unusual. Big breasted girls can be so unpretentious.

"My last name is Farmer, so if we got married your name would be Dairy Farmer."

I don't know what the hell made me say that. First I'm asking her for her last name like some kind of stalker, than I'm talking marriage. If

I were outside myself witnessing how bad I was screwing up instead of performing the screw-up, I'd probably kick me in the crotch.

"Is your last name really Farmer?"

"Yes," I said, taking the last sip of beer from the bottle I was holding to keep from saying, 'And I want to be the Farmer in the Dell,' which even in my present state, I knew would have been a deal breaker.

"Wow!"

"We both have agricultural names. We people of the land have to stick together. Let me buy you a drink and tell you all about me."

I bought her a drink and I bought one for myself so she wouldn't have to drink alone. I did tell her about myself, as promised. I also found out about her. She worked as an accountant. Like me, she'd graduated from college four years earlier. She told me a whole bunch of other things

I promptly forgot. I do remember thinking at the time that if her personality were a thing, it would be velvet.

Chapter 11

I was working in my office. It was late and dark outside. The school was as quiet as it could be. From time to time I could hear a muffled bang, the distant rumble of the boilers lighting, a ringing phone in the office. Amid these noises I heard the office door open. I didn't get up. I figured it was the night custodian coming for the garbage.

"Mr. Farmer?"

I looked up. "Oh hi Mrs. Vowel. I didn't know anyone was still here."

It was the eleventh grade English teacher. She was around my age, short and dumpy. She had blonde hair which, for some reason, had bleached highlights. She was good for English but not much else. Her husband was a cop which for some reason she mentioned in nearly every conversation.

"I was wondering if you could help me."

"Whatsup?"

"My laptop was stolen."

Actually it wasn't her laptop. It belonged to the school and given that we had no money for anything, it was quite a privilege, and a responsibility to be given a laptop to use.

"When was it taken?"

"I'm not sure. I don't use it much, just for the school newspaper. The last time I used it was Tuesday and I just noticed it missing. I don't know how it was taken. I always lock my door."

"Did you keep it locked in your closet?"

"No."

Of course not. Why would you follow school policy just because you were paid to do so? Why would you give a shit about something of value to a bunch of poor kids in an inner city school?

"I kept it on a file cabinet near my desk."

So here it is Friday night, I am very near the end of one hell of a long week and this, this . . . *English teacher*, informs me that she screwed up and I will likely spend hours looking through three days of videotape. But here's the best part.

"Well, I have to get going. I have to make dinner for my husband. Good night," she said, then turned and exited stage left. She walked out without a care in the world. Must be nice.

I started to ponder all the possibilities and decided to organize my investigation on the assumption that the teacher is an idiot. I figured that would save time.

I went to Mrs. Vowel's room first and checked the laptop's last known whereabouts, e.g. the file cabinet. It wasn't there nor was it in the closet, under her desk, in her desk or anywhere else real obvious. I was however, a little disappointed in myself in that I hadn't thought to check her car before she left.

I decided to narrow down the time frame the computer was stolen. I consulted the repository of all institutional knowledge with respect to actual happenings-the custodians. At the very least I might be able to save myself some time watching videotapes.

I consulted with Boots, the senior nighttime custodian. I have no idea why but everybody called him Boots. He was a tall, thin man of good disposition, but you had to be real careful how you talked to him because he had an I.Q. so low that, had it been converted into a belt size, that belt wouldn't fit a Barbie doll.

Boots didn't have any immediate information for me but later he stopped by my office while I was just starting to call up the videotape from the computer.

Our cameras didn't actually use videotape, they connected to a security company computer and everything was stored there for two weeks. I could, with the proper coordinates, call up any happening so long as I did so within two weeks of said occurrence.

There was one other restriction to the camera system: the cameras sucked. Apple, true to form, figured as he was getting cameras, who cared if they worked or not? A lot of cheap cameras beats a few effective cameras. He wasn't wrong in that, the board never checked the setup and they were impressed that we had cameras all over the place. The fact that they sucked was immaterial.

Boots said, "Hey-ya Mr. Farmer, I found this in the bathroom down by the gym."

He held up the carry case which formerly held the laptop. I began to be hopeful.

"Isn't that bathroom only open during games?" I asked.

"Yeah, I cleaned it last night after the game. Somebody used it today. They left shit in the bowl and I know I done cleaned it last night."

So the laptop had to have been stolen sometime today. That narrows it down. I said, "Mr. Boots you just saved me a bunch of time. You are a gentleman sir and I would say that next to me, you're the best."

"Thank you kindly Mr. Farmer. I's jes glad ta help."

So the culprit went into a locked room, stole a computer, walked all the way down the main hallway, then went into a locked bathroom, removed the laptop from its carry case, had a bowel movement, [I hope] he or she washed their hands, then left the building.

I immediately decided to name the entire matter "The Case of the Crapper." But giving it a clever moniker, and it was clever, was the easy part. Finding out the Crapper's identity and proving his or her guilt wasn't going to be easy.

I stayed and worked over the tapes for two hours. It wasn't just the cost of the computer, which to a poor district is considerable, motivating me. It was that we couldn't afford to have the kids think that such a theft is possible under current conditions at Sunnydale. If they started to believe we were the gang that couldn't shoot straight, we were sunk.

On Monday morning I was in Apple's office with the theory of the crime all ready to go. He came in and I told him what had happened. I could see he wasn't happy. I knew he was thinking that the superintendent wouldn't be happy, but I calmed him by telling him I had the crime as good as solved.

He wedged his bulk behind his desk and I stood near him as I set his computer to the right time and date in the security window.

"The video from our cameras is usually pretty bad but this is the worst," I said, temporarily forgetting he was the reason for said cameras.

Apple said nothing about my inadvertent dig. He was too busy calculating how this would go with the superintendent.

"The cameras kept cutting out at the worst times and the outside cameras were offline during this whole incident," I continued, more than happy to get past my faux pas. "This kid must have had a magnet in his head. If you watch you can see you walking down the hall."

On the video replay you could see Apple lurching and swaying down the hall, his ratty sport coat swaying in the effort. He was walking away from the ceiling mounted camera down the hall towards the double doors that led to the breezeway and the district office beyond.

"Then I noticed Lafayette, A.K.A. The Crapper, hanging around Mrs. Vowel's room door. Here's where the video camera cuts out."

"The Crapper?" Apple asked with a look of confusion.

"It's all part of the case," I assured him. "But look close, you can see it's Lafayette."

Lafayette was a tall black kid with a slight lisp, effeminate mannerisms and an afro that shot up and back from his rather high forehead at such an odd angle it looked like a party balloon emerging from his head. He was at his locker when Apple passed him but then he went over to Mrs. Vowel's door.

The video skipped so that all one could see was Lafayette standing by the door, then, instantly, he was much closer to the camera walking down the hall a good distance from the door.

"Now watch as he passes under the camera. See that?"

"What?"

"That glare."

"What glare?"

Lafayette was wearing a wildly oversized coat, which was not suspicious in and of itself since lots of our students wore them, but there was the tiniest flash in the lower left hand corner of the screen as he passed beneath the camera.

I rewound the part in question. "Right there," I said to an obviously bewildered Apple. "Well it doesn't matter. I believe that little reflection is from the buckle on the carry case to the laptop. He has it under his coat."

"That little bitty flash? That's not much to hang your hat on."

"Maybe, but I have one other bit of incriminating evidence."

"What else?"

"That was camera three. Now watch from camera four as he walks down the hall towards the lavatory."

I cued up the film from camera four and it showed Lafayette walking down the long hall. Just as he passed the main office doors, he looks back over his left shoulder.

"He's checking to see if anyone is on to what he is doing."

"You're nuts."

"Yes, but I'm also right on it."

"How are you going to get him to admit that he did it?"

"You mean, do I have a play wherein I'll catch the conscience of the Crapper? Don't worry, I got a plan."

I knew that catching the Crapper with the little evidence I had was not going to be easy, but it occurred to me that even though my analysis was based on some questionable evidence, *he* didn't know that. And like the man said, all warfare is based on deception. I decided to set up a bluff.

The downside to my bluff plan was that I had to enlist the help of a one Detective Sneer. I hated the guy. He was a sleazy climber who turned everything our students did into a federal case so he could impress his bosses.

My first contact with him was just inside the third week of school. He called to ask me if I knew who was on the basketball team. I told him that I could easily find out. He wanted to know, who was number twenty-nine? I called Biffy and she gave me the kid's name. I think it was the only time she gave me any assistance that whole year. He thanked me and hung up.

About a half an hour later, four heavily armed policemen and Sneer walk into my office, shut the door and then draw the little blind on the door window. I thought for a second they were there to work me over or something. I quickly calculated my odds of getting out of the ridiculously small, square window of my office before the cops could stop me. They weren't good.

Sneer stepped over to me and put out his hand. "Detective Sneer, Sunnydale P.D."

"Harris Farmer, Assistant Principal, Loyal American."

He was in his mid forties. He had a pot belly and the fat rolls bunched up at his shirt collar made him look like a humanoid Sharpe'. Worst of all he was wearing a checked shirt with a striped tie. I hate that look.

Given that the Detective and his boys had the drop on me, and I wasn't quite sure if they weren't there to beat me to a pulp, I quite forgot to make a mental note to wash my hands.

I sat down. Sneer and his henchman remained standing. "What can I do for you?" I asked.

"We're here to arrest the kid from the basketball team I called you about. Do you know what class he's in?"

"It's third lunch and he's a senior, he should be in the lunch room. May I ask why you want to arrest him?"

"He stole a car last night. He was wearing his basketball jersey. We know he did it,"

Sneer said. He had a reedy voice that made him seem even sleazier.

"Okay," I said slowly and thought for a second. "I'm not well versed in law enforcement but I know a little something about schools, I'd prefer not to have a riot here. Why don't I go down to the cafeteria and get the student to come back here and you can do the deed here out of the public eye?"

He thought for a second. My sharp mind could see that behind his beady little eyes, his Cro-Magnon brain was working out the odds I was going to tip the kid off and help him to escape. What an ass.

The last thing I needed was this guy and his four very white goons marching into the lunch room and doing a Rodney King number on a kid who, even if he was guilty, was guilty of being intensely stupid in the commission of a nonviolent crime. Hardly reason for the full court press the cops wanted to make it.

Once he figured I probably could be trusted, he agreed to the deal. I went to the cafeteria and found the kid. He was wearing his basketball jersey which would have been funny if I wasn't about to turn him over to the Heat.

I asked him to come to the office with me please. He nodded and got up from his lunch. When we got in the cross hall between the cafeteria and the main hallway he asked me what was up. I told him I'd rather discuss it in my office.

I walked in the office first. The cops had positioned themselves along the walls on both sides of the door so he couldn't see them till he was in the room. They were on him before he could twitch a muscle. I looked the kid straight in the eyes and shook my head ever so slightly communicating, 'Don't resist.' Then when I saw him open his mouth to say something, I said, like I was angry with him so the cops wouldn't figure out what I was doing, "This isn't the time to say anything, son!"

The kid, to his credit, picked up on my signal and didn't resist and didn't say a word. The atmosphere in that room was charged. Those cops were ready to do battle and Sneer was there with his pad out to write down anything they could use against the kid. The kid was wise to heed my warning.

But I could see the other side to it. Someone called about their car being robbed and the big bad detective wanted to get credit for capturing such a dangerous fiend. He was a kid who stole a car for a joy ride. There was no need to call out the cavalry. But since the cavalry was called out it made Sneer's part all that much more spectacular.

Sneer made me hate him. He would beat up on poor black kids to get ahead if necessary. I don't know what pissed me off most, his racism, his hatred for the poor, or his total disregard for responsible duty.

In any case, I loathed bringing him in but I needed him to make my plan to solve the Case of the Crapper work. For if it failed, the Crapper would escape justice and the school would be out a whole laptop computer and most of the next edition of the school newspaper. It would also encourage the criminal element at Sunnydale.

Sneer showed up at my door, this time without his posse. He was wearing a white shirt with brown pants. I almost never wore brown. I didn't like the way I looked in brown. This guy always wore brown, another good reason to dislike him.

"Hey! Detective Sneer, thanks for coming down."

"What's this all about?"

I quickly filled Detective Sneer in on all the particulars of the case. And although my conversations with him always had the feel of trying to hold on to a greased eel, I sensed he understood and wanted to participate in my honestly deceptive plan.

"So you see? I just need you to play along," I finished up.

He chuckled. "Okay, I guess I could help you out. But if this doesn't work you won't get a second chance at this kid and you can kiss the computer goodbye."

"I know. It'll work."

I was seated behind my desk when Lafayette came to my office. Detective Sneer was standing, as per our arrangement, in the back of the office behind the two chairs in front of my desk.

"You wanted to see me Mr. Farmer?"

"Yeah, hey Lafayette, come on in and sit down."

I waited till he sat down and then I got up and closed the door. I walked back to my chair and sat down slowly.

After I settled in the chair I looked Lafayette in the eyes, waited a beat, and then said, "I need the computer back."

"What computer?"

"The computer you took."

"Mr. Farmer there is no way I took a computer. I would never do that! Seriously, I have-,"

I cut him off. I dropped my voice in pitch and drawled, "I know that you took it. I watched you do it on the video cameras so don't insult me by telling me you didn't do it."

He didn't say anything. He just stared for a second.

"Mr. Farmer I swear I didn't take that computer. You can ask anyone. I-,"

"I don't need to ask anyone, I know you took it because I saw you do it. I have the whole thing on videotape. I need the computer back. It has a great deal of work on it for the school newspaper."

He was going to say something. I could see he was trying to decide what tack to take next. The wheels were spinning.

I waited just enough time for maximum effect, then said the line on which my whole plan rested. It would be the pivotal point in this battle of wits. It was the whole reason I asked Sneer to be there. I said, "If I don't get it back I am going to turn the case over to the detective here and he won't be as understanding as I am."

Lafayette took a long look at Detective Sneer standing behind him. Sneer, according to my plan, said nothing and did nothing. He just stood there looking scary, his gun and handcuffs clearly visible on his belt.

The moment got heavy on Lafayette's shoulders. It pressed down till he blurted, "I did it. I took the computer."

"Where is the computer now?"

"It's at home."

I got up and went to the file cabinet next to him and got a yellow legal pad that was sitting on top. I put it on the edge of the desk in front of him.

"Lafayette, I want you to write down everything that happened with this computer thing. Make sure you date and sign it. . . . Oh Yeah, when you're done I want you to give me the key you used."

Lafayette looked up at me in shock. He didn't think I knew about the key. But I knew he had to have one. Even though the video cut out, the time signatures before and after the cut indicated that he had gotten in the room through the locked door, got the computer, positioned it under his coat and was out the door in less than eighty seconds. There is no way he did that without a key.

In the end, I got the key and his confession. And so I solved the Case of the Crapper and I naively thought it was behind me. But then, nothing is above politics in school districts.

The very next day I was in my office and the phone rang. I picked it up and answered, "Harris Farmer, Assistant Principal Extraordinaire."

It was His Majesty the Superintendent. "Hey Harris, you working hard?"

He always called me Harris but I had to call him Dr. Mayonnaise. It was the big chair thing all over again.

"Oh yeah, I've been working harder than a dentist's drill at a candy convention."

Rumplestilsken spun straw into gold. Superintendents spin reality into bullshit. Bullshit is like gold to them.

"Did you handle the laptop theft?"

"Yes, I did. I called his mom and she brought it back. Unfortunately, he erased most of the next issue of the school newspaper," I reported, proud of myself for my ingenuity.

"Did you notify the police yet?"

"Yes. I made a report to the police and turned over his signed confession to them."

I also had the computer guy for the school, Brannon, make a back up of the entire hard drive for evidence. It seems Lafayette, in the time it took me to catch him, had downloaded a shitload of gay porn. I didn't tell his mother, or anyone for that matter, about the porn and I had no intention of bringing that into it but I wanted the evidence if it did come up. Snarky, I know.

I don't have a bias toward homosexuality, but even if I did I don't believe educators should judge students in that way. All too often educators forget that the object is not to tell students specifically how to live but rather to give them the tools to make good choices in dealing with the lives they will lead. Even if it were possible to indoctrinate students in the way many want, it would never prepare the students for ever changing circumstance.

As far as I was concerned, if Lafayette wanted to look at gay porn, that was his choice to make, but it is unacceptable to steal property and interfere with the hard work of his peers on the school newspaper. My responsibility here was to teach him that there were consequences for such behavior.

After all, I had standing orders to report any thefts to the police but I didn't have any instructions insofar as sexual orientation was concerned. But even if I had, I had no intention of getting Lafayette estranged from his mother or beaten by the other students.

Along the same line, any teacher found to be a homosexual can be fired. No questions asked. That's why no matter what I felt about a teacher I never said a word, nor did I ever engage in gossip on the subject.

I figured Dr. Mayonnaise would prefer not to know. But I sensed there was something wrong. I thought I heard him give a short sigh.

"Is there something wrong?" I asked.

"No," he said, which meant 'Hell yes.'

Now I was perplexed. Certainly, I had

done a good job. Surely, I was to be rewarded with praise and possibly a feast in my honor. But I wasn't hearing that.

"It's just, we should have considered what we were going to do before the police were involved."

"Perhaps," I said, starting to sweat a little, "but it is our policy to report all such thefts to the police. That computer cost nearly two thousand dollars."

"Yes," he said, which in Admin-speak, a language unique to school administrators, meant, 'You fucked up royal!'

There was a huge 'but' coming and I braced myself for it. He paused a second then asked with a breezy tone, as if he were changing the subject which he was most certainly not, "Did you know that this young man is Lou's nephew?"

Oh shit, I thought as my heart dropped

into my stomach. So that's what this was. I wasn't supposed to have treated Lou's nephew the same as everyone else even though Lou frequently lectured us during school board meetings to "Keep the discipline fair."

It was a crystal clear case of don't do as I say, do as I not say but really mean. How could I have missed that point? As an outsider of Sunnydale I was not quite up to speed on all the complex family trees of the players. I guess I should have asked Lafayette who he was related to before I proceeded with my investigation of him.

"No, I didn't know that," I said.

"Well next time check with me first, okay?" he said almost genially. He was happy. The pressure was off him. My stating that I didn't know the kid was Lou's nephew took Mayonnaise off the hook. He could easily deflect any blame my way.

"Okay, I'll talk to you later," I said.

"Bye."

I hung up and called Apple right away.

"Hey, it's me Harris Farmer. You're not going to believe this. I just got off the phone with the Superintendent. I think he's pissed because I turned the Crapper over to the Fuzz."

"Who?"

"The kid who stole the computer. He's the nephew of a one Lou Mustard."

He thought about it for a minute, "Step over to my office."

"Yeah, Okay, I'll be there in like five minutes."

Four minutes later I went to his office. He was drinking out of a huge bottle of fruit juice. He frequently substituted fruit juice for food during the daylight hours but would eat a quantity of meat somewhere in the vicinity of half a cow for dinner. It was a unique diet that he whole heartedly believed in but which didn't work at all. Yet, he thought I was nuts for being a vegetarian.

"You were right. The superintendent is pissed."

"Oh man."

"I just got off the phone with him."

"Damn!"

"Next time check with me before you do something like that."

"I don't believe this. I got the confession, the key and the computer back. And somehow I'm the bad guy? I feel like I fell through the looking glass."

"Hey, I know. Just don't worry about it. He's nuts. He'll get over it. But you'd better be careful. Lou's out to get you now."

"For doing my job!?"

Apple just shrugged his shoulders. He

didn't exactly have a brand in this fire but there was something about watching me go down that had an entertaining appeal to him. I have no doubt that of all the Romans in the coliseum, he would have been cheering the loudest when the Christians were being eaten by lions.

You'd better believe Lou was out to get me. Now I was confused. It seemed that because I was so busy trying to do my job right I had screwed up by doing it right. I didn't see that one coming.

Chapter 12

Several of my snitches informed me that there was a conspiracy to commit a food fight during first lunch. I immediately held a council of war with Rick and Principal Apple. We decided to go to the cafeteria and keep the wheels turning. That is, circulate and make sure the students dump their trays as soon as they finish with their lunch.

Most students don't eat everything they get at lunch. Much of it goes in the trash. Students will eat what they want then leave the tray in front of them while they converse with their friends or play a game or read. All that food they're taking their time about disposing of is ammunition for a food fight. We didn't want a replay of the food fight that happened in the first month of school, which I later determined was started by the teachers, one in particular.

The Sunnydale cafeteria was not large enough for the school itself. The result was that we had to have three lunch periods-hell on scheduling. The seventh and eighth grades were given first lunch.

The kitchen served two lunch lines, a small consolation since the women who worked there were in their mid nineties and couldn't move fast at all. There was a mini serving area on the wall opposite the kitchen which basically served junk food kindly referred to as "snacks." Naturally, the students loved it.

Knowing that the students were junk food junkies the teachers decided to use that against them. They would order the small kiosk closed if the students misbehaved. I wasn't opposed to this necessarily, but I did tell the lead lunchroom teacher not to overdo it.

Any punishment, as I told her, loses effectiveness if the punished perceive it to be abusive. That line is crossed with students when the punishment goes on so long that they forget what initiated it in the first place. I told her that as annoying as it may be, you have to reset the clock every now and then. In other words, you have to move past the infraction, start over and allow the students to go back to business as usual.

This stupid bitch, who was always angry about something and had a sense of entitlement because she had a brother on the school board and a brother who was the athletic director, had closed the kiosk for two weeks. The kids got pissed and decided to retaliate. I have to admit that after the principal yelled at the entire two grades, which he had me bring to the auditorium for that purpose, after I suspended thirty-five students and after nearly twenty-five hours of labor were wasted on the whole affair, I wanted to throw food at her too.

Naturally, I didn't want a repeat, and by close monitoring, and by removing the "extra" food from the tables, I was hoping another food fight could be avoided. Rick and Apple each took a garbage can on wheels around the cafeteria for the kids to throw their food remains in. I had no intention of touching a garbage can, much less stand next to one in a silk suit at the mercy of the student's aim and the viscosity of the various juices and liquids inherent in the sugarfest that was lunch.

I walked up and down the rows of tables and each time I spotted students who looked as if they were done I would say, "Hey if you guys are done, let's clean it up."

One girl named Moniesha asked, "Hey Mr. Farmer, what the Principal and Mr. Bird be doing here today?"

"I don't know Moniesha, . . maybe they're hungry."

Another girl named Triease asked, "Hey Mr. Farmer, there gonna be a food fight today?"

"Nah Triease, that's just a rumor started by rumor starters," I lied. They knew exactly what was going on. They wanted to see how I handled it. Funny thing was, I felt closer to them when they were on the verge of tearing the place apart. Maybe it was because I wanted to do the same thing.

A girl named Drucy walked up to me. "Mr. Farmer, how come Mr. Apple be here?"

"He's here to make sure I don't eat too much. Apparently some of you students complained that I was fat," I said, with mock indignation.

She laughed at that and shook her head then went back to her friends to report what and how the transaction transpired.

I looked back across the cafeteria and I could see Apple arguing with Alejandro Sanchez. They were both gesticulating wildly but with the noise of the students banging off every surface I couldn't hear a word of what they were arguing about. I figured it was Alejandro getting into yet another dispute with one of his peers. The kid didn't discriminate, he fought with his friends as much as his enemies.

I turned to look for more students finished with their lunch but had not yet disposed of the leftover detritus. I found a few more, did my thing then looked over to check the Principal and Alejandro. They were both gone.

That interchange between Sanchez and the Principal was the big happening that day. There was no food fight, either because we foiled it or the information from my snitches was not accurate. At the risk of being the sort of guy I would ordinarily criticize, I will opt for the headline "Food Fight Foiled, Assistant Principal Declared Hero." Insofar as the altercation between Mr. Sanchez and Mr. Apple goes, there was much more to it but, I wasn't to find that out till later.

Things rolled on; going from one dispute to another and later that afternoon I was in my office when Mr. White stepped in to talk to me.

"Are you busy?"

"I'm always busy, but don't let that stop you. What can I do for you?"

I always kept the door to my office open, literally and figuratively. I have worked with administrators who acted as if they were the great and powerful Oz. As in, 'Nobody gets to see [them], not no way, not no how.' But I never liked that and given that human interaction is the work of schools, it didn't make much sense to me. Get to the problem before it is a problem, is a strategy that lives on information. And how much information can you get if you don't talk to people?

"Did you get that write-up I put in your box about the kid with the flag?" White asked.

"I did see you wrote something about a kid running around the room and dropping a book but I didn't get a chance to read the whole thing."

"This kid wouldn't stop. First he threw a student's book in the garbage can and wouldn't get it out. Then he was running around the room and wouldn't sit down. Then he was playing with the flag. He was unhinged."

I picked up the small mountain of referrals sitting on my desk. The teachers at Sunnydale wrote-up students for just about everything. I flipped through them and found the one White had written. It was unusual for a substitute teacher to write up kids. Typically, they didn't care enough about what happened either way.

"The kid's name is Ted Brown?"

"Yeah, I think that's it," he said.

"I know him. He doesn't get in trouble much.

"I want him punished."

"I'm on it."

"Thanks."

Just after he left I picked up the phone and punched the numbers to my pseudo secretary.

The conversation from my end sounded like this, "Hello Biffy? Well who is this? Where is Biffy? Did she come to work at all today? How about this week? Forget that. Listen, I need to see a student named Ted Brown. Please have him come to my office. Thank You."

A few minutes later Ted Brown stood at the doorway to my office and knocked lightly. He was a well-mannered ninth grader who was tall, thin and had smooth good looks that I could see he was used to using to his advantage.

"Hey, thanks for coming down," I said, rising. "Come on in and sit down."

He walked in slowly and sat in one of the chairs in front of my desk.

"I just wanted to ask you how things were going," I said sitting down.

"Okay."

"No, problems with anything?"

"No, everything is awright," he said, looking over the office. He may have never been in there before. He wasn't the sort who got in trouble much.

"What about the other day in Spanish class with Mr. White?"

"He got mad cause I accidentally dropped a book in the garbage," he said, with almost no emotion.

"Accidentally?"

"Yeah, I was playing with it then I dropped it by accident."

"What were you doing out of your seat with another student's book?"

"I was messin around."

"What about refusing to sit down?"

"I didn't refuse. I sat down eventually."

"But you did run around the room?"

"Yeah, I was just messin around."

"Here's what I think, and you tell me if I'm wrong. I think you were bored or maybe a little out of sorts and you had a substitute teacher so you decided to give the guy a hard time."

"Yeah."

"You're not like that ordinarily. You never get in trouble."

"Yeah, I know, I was just messin around. It won't happen again."

"That's fine with me, but the demands of justice must be met. That's why I am going to give you two days in-school suspension."

"I gotta do two days ISS?! Man, that ain't fair!"

"How do you figure? You just said yourself you were giving the guy a hard time deliberately."

"That's because I was mad at him."

"What were you mad at him about?"

"He said I should go back to Africa."

"He said that?"

"Yeah."

"That's really insulting. Why did he say that?"

Now, I do not believe a word of this. If Old Man White had said something so offensive and if Ted was as offended as he claimed, that would have been the first thing out of his mouth. Instead, he didn't mention it until I told him he was getting time in ISS. Besides which, Mr. White ain't the kind. But then, when it comes to race relations, America is totally batshit.

"Well, I said I didn't like the flag and he said, 'Then why don't you go back to Africa?'"

"What makes him think your family comes from Africa anyway? You could have come from South America or any number of other places for that matter."

"Well I don't like people talking to me dat way. I got angry."

"Well, why don't we put the whole ISS thing on hold till I get to the bottom of things?"

I have to look into this but I don't want this guy contaminating the witness pool and the In-School Suspension room is an information hub the CIA would be proud to call their own.

"I'm going to speak with Mr. White."

Later, when I did talk to Mr. White, I stated the matter in the least shocking way I could think of and the guy still looked as if I had told him the most shocking thing in the world.

"I never said that! We were waiting by the door waiting for the bell and he said he hated the flag and I said, 'Why don't you leave the country then?'"

"I see."

"I never even said the word 'Africa!'"

"Okay. I understand what you're saying. To be honest with you I didn't really buy the kid's story anyway. However, I am going to need to check it out. Do me a favor and don't mention it to anyone."

My intention was to gather the testimony of witnesses and I knew their answers would be more candid if they didn't know what I am asking about. I didn't want Mr. White or Ted talking.

"Okay. But I would never say something like that. I worked with black people for years when I was an engineer for General Electric. I had-,"

"Relax Mr. White. You don't have to recount your bona fides with me. I don't believe you are a racist, but you understand that I have to take such accusations seriously. If I don't paint by the numbers on this one I'm going to have more trouble than a sweet piece of cheese like me deserves."

He probably wasn't a racist in the classic sheet wearing sense. Very few of those types would even accept a job at Sunnydale in the first place. But racism comes in many subtle colors and given the titanic amount of racism African Americans face, such a charge bears scrutiny. So I scrutinized it.

Chapter 14

Not long after Mr. White left, Alejandro Sanchez entered my office with his step-father, Mr. Moss. Mr. Moss had to be at least twenty years older than Alejandro's mother. He was a big man with a large belly, jowls that oscillated when he talked and sparse white hair.

I usually did not get friendly or even on a first name basis with parents. I didn't want familiarity to compromise my objectivity; besides, I wasn't there to make friends. But I did like Mr. Moss. He worked over at the steel mill.

"Mr. Farmer, you got a minute?"

"Always for you Mr. Moss. How's the foot? I see you don't have the crutches anymore."

Some young dope at the steel mill had prematurely tapped a blast furnace and caused molten steel to pour into Mr. Moss' boot. The kid was lucky Moss didn't shove what was left of his foot up his ass.

"It's fine, but I'm mad."

"About what?"

"Before, in the cafeteria, Mr. Apple attacked my son."

"He what!?" I blurted. Now I knew how Mr. White felt.

Alejandro, on the verge of tears said, "John Gray was bustin on me so I hit him in the back of the head-,"

"He was wrong to hit the Gray boy but that's not the point," Mr. Moss interjected.

"Yeeeah, he had no right to be grabbin me!"

I had to put a stop to this spiral. These two guys were feeding off each other's anger like wind and fire on a tire dump. "Why don't you both have a seat?"

They both caught their breath and took a seat. I could see Mr. Moss was still favoring his injured foot. The guy was tough.

"Are you saying the Principal grabbed you?"

"Yeeeeah!" Alejandro screeched, going right back to near hysterical. "He grabbed me and dragged me to the door. Then he slammed me up against the door jamb. He ain't got no right to be touching me!"

"I don't want the principal roughing up my son. I know he's no angel, but this is wrong. I'm going to the cops."

I definitely didn't want this guy going to the cops before I even knew what the hell they were talking about. I'm guessing this had something to do with the thing in the lunch room.

The first order of business in such a situation is to find out with some degree of certainty what the hell happened. Students and the adults can be quite loose with the facts, especially if emotions are running high.

Once I had a student come to my office and tell me that the teacher slammed him up against his locker when they had a dispute in the hallway. The "dispute" was about him going to his locker while on a trip to the lavatory, a clear violation of the rules, and the teacher told him he couldn't do that. I guess the kid was so busy plotting his revenge on the teacher he didn't take notice of the camera in the ceiling ten feet away.

The student came in the next day with his mother. He raged, cried and railed at the indignity of it all. His mother wanted the teacher fired. I told her I was perfectly prepared to do that but I wanted her to take a look at the video tape before we came to that decision.

The tape was without sound but it showed her son giving the teacher a hard time and at no time did the teacher stand within eight feet of the kid. The mom was pissed and I could feel the vibration from the fury boiling inside her. Instead of getting the Oscar nomination for Best Portrayal of an Abused Student, he got an ass whooping.

In this instance, the one wherein Alejandro accused the Principal of battery, I needed to find out more information. I also needed to cool down Alejandro.

"Hey Alejandro could you wait outside for me? I need to confer with your dad, okay?"

"Yeah okay," he said and shuffled out the door to wait in the main office.

"Mr. Moss I'm going to be honest with you. I have no idea what happened here. I can't believe Principal Apple would abuse your son. But, I would ask you to hold off on calling the police till I talk with the principal and get back to you."

I believed Apple capable of anything but I didn't believe he would be so stupid as to do anything that would get him fired so fast.

"Well . . . I guess so."

"I will call you end of business today to let you know what I come up with, I promise. Alejandro seems upset so if you want to take him home for the rest of the day I understand."

I was offering to let the kid go home because I did believe he was upset, he wouldn't do any learning in that condition and he would most probably prevent others from learning by acting out in some fashion. I also didn't want him marching around making his tale of woe public knowledge before I had a plan to deal with it.

"Yeah, I'll take him home."

"I will fix it in CompuSchool. Don't worry, it won't affect his attendance."

He nodded, still not quite sure if he'd done the right thing in trusting the matter to me rather than going straight to the cops. I guessed that he really didn't want to, or he would have gone there first. He came to me instead of the principal because he wanted me to do the work of the conflict for him.

In truth, there was not a whole lot I could do. If Apple didn't do it I would have to prove a negative. If he did do it, I couldn't fire him or even reprimand him. The most I could do would be to tattle to the superintendent.

My best course of action here would be to make this someone else's problem, just walk away. The only problem with that option was the school and ultimately the students pay when cops, judges and lawyers get involved. If there is one law of nature in the school universe which can always be relied upon, it is that once lawyers get involved with schools, nobody learns anything.

After Mr. Moss stepped out of the room I gave him three minutes to get out of the immediate vicinity then made a beeline to Apple's office. I found him, as usual, sitting behind his desk working on his first myocardial infarction. I closed the door before I took a seat. I didn't want anyone overhearing this conversation.

"Mr. Moss came to see me today."

"Who?"

Had it been Alejandro's mother, Apple would have remembered. She was in her early thirties and she had an amazing rack. She was well aware of her assets and always wore shirts that showcased those beautiful bumpers. It was damn hard not to stare at them. Once in her presence, it was all but impossible to forget them.

"The Sanchez kid's stepfather. He was pissed at you. He said you slammed his kid up against the door jamb as you led him out of the cafeteria."

"He's nuts. I grabbed his son because the kid was starting to fight with the other kid and refused to leave when I told him to. As I was walking him through the door he tripped and fell into the door jamb. If I wasn't holding him by the arm he would have been hurt worse."

"The kid does fight a lot. The only thing is, the old man wants to go to the cops. How do you want me to handle it? I could set up a meeting if you want."

"Nah, just talk to him and tell him what happened."

What he was really telling me was to make it go away. If this had happened with a teacher he would have insisted the teacher meet with one or both the parents. But since it was he who was on the hot seat, the bastard wanted me to handle it. That meant at the very least I was going to get yelled at by the parents.

"Got it," I said, making no indication as to how I felt and left.

That night I waited to call Mr. Moss. I even waited for most of the school personnel to drift off after school before I looked at the video tape. I didn't want anyone to know about this incident and I didn't want any interruptions while I scrutinized the tape.

There were two video cameras in the cafeteria. Both were located in the ceiling in front of the main doors and each faced one side of the cafeteria. In order to get the wide angle necessary for this setup, the security people had to put a special lens on those two cameras which gave the picture a fisheye effect as well as increased the distortion on the already grainy images. If I were ever to rob a bank, I want the bank to have cameras just like those two.

I could see Apple walk up to and past the camera. Alejandro was to the Principal's right and therefore the left side of the screen. The problem was that Alejandro was too short to be much in frame. All I could see was the very top of his head. I knew that was the best I was going to get because the cameras faced away from the doors. This was a he said/she said argument. It was the word of one person against another's.

I sighed and picked up the phone. I didn't want to make this call. I knew how it was going to go. I wasn't wrong.

"Hello?"

"Hey, Mr. Moss? This is Harris Farmer."

"Hello."

"I spoke with Mr. Apple and he assures me that he didn't slam Alejandro into the door, but rather Alejandro tripped as he was leading him out of the cafeteria."

"He shouldn't have touched him at all."

I dropped my voice into sympathetic mode and said, "Mr. Moss, nobody wants such things to happen but I don't think you and I would be discussing this had Alejandro left the cafeteria when the principal asked him to. Nobody here likes Alejandro more than I do but even I gotta admit he does fight with the other students a lot."

"I know he fights a lot but that don't mean he should be treated bad. Nobody has a right to put their hands on him." He was becoming angry again.

"I agree. I think you're right. I think Alejandro should be accorded the same treatment as everyone else." *And puppy dogs should all go to loving homes.*

"It's against the law for him to be grabbed up like that."

"Actually, it's not. We may employ physical means to maintain order. Nobody wants to do that but we have a big school to be responsible for."

I wasn't lying to him. School personnel may use physical force to maintain order if a given situation comes to it, but I would say that sort of thing shouldn't be necessary. However, I am not blind to the fact that the behavior of students has gotten worse every year I've been in education.

In one school I worked at there was an ancient Math teacher who had worked nearly fifty years as a teacher. His name was Mr. McFee. He was a short, exceedingly thin man who looked like he would break in half if anyone sneezed on him. I called him Mr. McFeeble.

One day I was talking to McFeeble and he remarked that student behavior hadn't changed one bit since he had become a teacher nearly five decades before. I questioned him about this remark, pointing out some of my observations on the subject and after a short while he recanted and admitted that they had indeed changed for the worse.

Maybe McFeeble was just creating nostalgia to sustain him while he ran out the clock to his retirement and if that is the case, I was a total shithead to say anything. But his willingness to overlook the obvious facts to obtain a little personal comfort is what bothered me. All too many people in education are willing to sacrifice any drive for excellence and let sleeping dogs lie so long as doing so suits their comfortable position.

What Mr. Moss didn't get is that in a battle of veracity, his son's terrible record was going to work against him. The kid had a hell of a discipline record.

"He didn't have to shove my boy up against that door."

"Principal Apple assures me that the boy tripped. I must tell you that I have never known Mr. Apple to be a violent man. I seriously doubt-,"

Mr. Moss cut me off shouting, "You're just covering up for him! You're all alike! You don't care! I'm goin to the police!"

"Mr. Moss-,"

"Go to hell!" he screamed and slammed the phone down.

I slumped in my chair feeling like I was the only person left on the planet earth. "No problem . . .I'll get on that right away," I said, slowly laying the handset down in its carriage.

Chapter 14

Schools are always in motion and more happens inside any given school on any given day than any one administrator can process. A good school leader, and they are scarcer than hen's teeth, guides that motion in positive directions.

Yet monitoring what was going on was crucial in steering. One of the ways I gathered information was through banter. It is amazing what you can learn in seemingly casual conversation.

My problem at Sunnydale was that none of the people above me or below me seemed to want me to do anything positive. They all had their own little agendas and the school mission be damned.

These two thoughts of school leadership and cooperative allies collided in my head when I discovered a little something-something disturbing about one of our teachers during a routine chat with one of my more reliable snitches. It was a dark shape on the horizon I wanted to get nowhere near alone, so I thought my best bet would be to solicit the help of Rick Bird, a man with a moral center and no discernable agenda.

I went to his office and found him in conversation with Ms. Siren. Even though the door was slightly ajar I couldn't hear what they were talking about. I waited politely for them to finish.

After about three minutes Ms. Siren came walking out. "Hi, Mr. Farmer," she said.

"Hey, Ms. Siren."

I walked into Rick's office. His office was, as anyone would expect, neat as a pin. Once upon a time he was a science teacher and he had reminders of that all over his office in the form of geodes, posters of nebulae on the walls and a tall trophy he had received from some organization for being a great science teacher.

Rick came to Sunnydale because of love. Not a love of Sunnydale but the love of a woman, the most unfortunate kind of love. He was a beloved science teacher in a fairly affluent school district before he let his emotion cause what I consider a huge fall from grace.

Rick's district had hired a new superintendent and when she came around to introduce herself to everyone, Rick, being the nice guy that he was, invited her to join the science club in stargazing that night. She took him up on his offer and afterward, when the gear was all packed up and the last student departed, Rick, being the nice guy that he was, invited her for a drink.

They started to date and not long after that, they married. Rick had to seek employment elsewhere because it was considered a conflict of interest for him to be married to the head cheese. He left a job he loved, in a district he loved, to work at Sunnydale.

As much as I admired and respected Rick, I couldn't ever forgive his marrying a superintendent. Our school board hated Rick. I was never able to find out specifically what it was they disliked about him and when I asked Apple about it, he told me that it was because the board disliked all the administrators. He said they were nuts.

"What's with her?" I asked as I took a seat in front of Rick's desk.

"Oh, she was having some trouble with a few students making lewd remarks."

"Ya know, it could be because she is so attractive, but there could be more to the story. In fact, she's the reason I came in here to talk to you."

"What do you mean?"

"I don't know for sure, but I have been hearing some strange things from some strange students. If this woman is, shall we say, becoming overly-friendly with a student or two, it would have an effect on discipline."

"What have you heard?"

"I heard she was hanging around with a group of students at a student's house after school. I also heard she was out in front of the movie theater with a student. I was not able to find anyone to confirm she actually went into the movies with a student. But, I did get the feeling that I was not being told the whole story, like the kids were holding something back."

"You think she is becoming overly friendly?"

"I don't know but if we see smoke can we afford to not check to see if there is a fire? It's possible these kids are making lewd comments because they are just idiots, but it is also possible they're getting bold because they know something about this woman. You have to admit this school has one hell of a coconut telegraph."

"Okay, suppose you are right. What do we do?"

"I've seen this sort of thing before."

I am ashamed to say it has happened at every school I've ever worked in. Although, few of the perpetrators were female and none of them as good looking as Ms. Siren. But they were always there.

The whole thing was creepy to me. I never saw students in a sexual way. To me they were kids. But even if I did have a desire in that way I never would have pursued it. When you sex-up a child you commit a crime second only to murder, you steal their childhood. You cut short the greatest memory making time of their lives. It's unforgivable.

The weird thing is that schools only recently cracked down on the adults who go after the children. On my first teaching assignment I found out through a loose lipped guidance counselor that the school had had three teachers who were caught engaging in sexual activities with the students. Not one of the three child-fuckers was fired for what they'd done.

Through some diligent digging I was able to discover the identities of two of the three. I never did determine who the third man was and I often pondered if that was a lesson of sorts. Someday as a wizened administrator I could look at a young administrator and say, "You have to always be on the lookout for the third man."

Rick and I sat in silence considering our options. Finally, I said, "I would like to kick her ass out of the building right now but that might be a real problem if we are wrong. Why don't we ask our good friend the detective to do a quiet check for us?"

"Yeah, that sounds like a good idea. I'll tell Apple."

Man, I hated having to call Detective Sneer again but politics makes strange bedfellows, and if Ms. Siren indeed had strange bedfellows, I needed to find out to minimize the damage. As I dialed, I reminded myself that I was acting in the interest of the students and that is reason enough to ignore the hideous sensation of having snot-bugs crawling all over me.

"Detective Sneer," he said, as if he were a decent person.

"Hey, Detective Sneer, it's Harris Farmer, Assistant Principal, Weapon-of-mass-instruction. How you doing today?" I said as pleasantly as I could.

"Okay. What can I do for you?" he asked unenthusiastically. He wasn't buying. This guy knew I was calling to give him more work, and in addition to being a lazy shit, he also calculated that whatever it was, it wouldn't advance his career. Therefore, he didn't want any.

"Listen, we've been getting some strange vibes from some strange talk about one of our teachers. We were wondering if you could quietly check it out for us."

What I was doing was not cool. Calling the Klingons to investigate one of the workers' personal lives was something that went against my populist grain, but I justified my actions because the greater harm here was to a child. Still, nothing is harder for a liberal to do than to use the "ends justify the means" argument.

"What have you been hearing and who is the teacher?" he asked in a bored tone as if he were talking to a crazy housewife calling about the neighbor's cat shitting in her flowerbed.

Talk about humiliation. First I had to compromise some heartfelt values to do what I was doing, then I had to put up with the attitude of this arrogant ass. What was next? Giving Mr. Woods the Teacher of the Year Award?

"She's one of our math teachers. Her name is Ms. Siren. We've been hearing some talk, which admittedly, could just be a rumor she's been hanging out with students and doing who knows what."

"What did you want me to do?"

He knows damn well what to do but he's thinking ahead. He knows that if ever called on the carpet for investigating this person, he wants to be able to say, 'I was specifically asked to do it by one of the school administrators.' Or perhaps, more in tune with his type, 'I was only following orders.'

"We were hoping you could quietly check to see if our suspicions are correct. Hey, I hope we are wrong but we need to make sure."

I was jumping in with both feet with that last statement. It was on me now. If there were any repercussions for what we were doing they would land on me. It didn't bother me too much though. I understand that leadership involves risk and you can make yourself nuts as well as ineffectual if you focus too much on the downside.

"I understand. I'll check it out and get back to you," he said and hung up.

After I got off the phone with the detective I decided to attend to the White/Brown affair and do a little investigating of my own. The tough part of this type of information gathering is getting it done as quickly and quietly as possible so that the students don't get word through the telegraph. Stories can change dramatically if the participants have time to think about how certain alterations can benefit them.

I went through the class roster and picked out the names of people whom I thought would make good witnesses and several whom I thought would make bad witnesses.

I always used a variety of witnesses to guard against a charge of bias. I also did it just in case there was some bias. It's hard not to pick a side even though you set out to be objective. What if some part of me secretly favored the old man over the kid? Or, what if some part of me automatically picked the kid because of all the times I witnessed people being racist towards black people?

The students at Sunnydale were remarkable in describing the behaviors they witnessed, even though they were somewhat oblivious to their own behaviors. Perhaps it was due to the fact that since they had no wealth, their survival depended heavily on the personal relationships with family and community members. I was fairly certain I would be able to work out a clear picture of what actually happened through my interviews.

The first witness I talked to was a sixteen year old black girl named Rosa. She was an ace student and I had a good relationship with her. I called her to my office and she showed up right away.

"Rosa, what's the story with what happened the other day in Mrs. Wicker's class when Mr. White was subbing there?"

She looked confused for a second. I was being vague on purpose. I didn't want to lead the witness, and whether or not she would recall the incident specifically from the scant information I gave her in itself told me how big a deal it was.

"Oh yeah, Teddy was giving him a hard time. He was running around the classroom all actin the fool. And he threw a book in the trash. He was being a jerk."

"Did Mr. White say anything to him?"

Again I was being vague behind a logical question.

"Yeah he kept telling him to sit down and stop it and stuff."

"What happened with the flag as everyone was leaving?"

"What? Flag? Oh yeah! Teddy said, 'I hate this flag.' Then Mr. White said, 'Then why don't you leave the country?'"

"Mr. White didn't say anything about Africa?"

"No."

"Did Mr. White even say the word 'Africa?'"

Here, I was leading a little but I wanted it to be on the record. But just because Rosa, whom I believe to be a very reliable witness, didn't hear him say the word doesn't mean he didn't say it.

"No, some of the kids said something about Africa but I didn't hear them."

I thanked her and asked her not to discuss what we had talked about. I also got started on my other witnesses right away because I knew the shelf life of a secret at Sunnydale was shorter than a superintendent's conscience. Short indeed.

The interviews with the witnesses went pretty much the same. I asked no leading questions and got pretty much the same results.

" . . .I wasn't paying attention. But I didn't hear Mr. White say nothing about no Africa. He told the boy to sit down a lot a times though."

". . .Mr. White said, 'Why don't you leave if you don't like it?' and the students in the back all yelled 'Ooooooooowwwwww he said, Go back to Africa!' Mr. White never said anything about Africa."

". . . I was about three feet from Mr. White as we were waiting for the bell. He didn't say nothin about Africa."

The picture that emerged was that Teddy was misbehaving all over the place in that class. Mr. White should have kicked his ass out but didn't. During the last few minutes of class the students all gathered at the door to await the bell. Teddy started swiping at the flag, batting the bottom of it. He then said, "I hate this flag."

Mr. White said, "Then why don't you leave the country?"

Mr. White had served in the Navy and applied to go to Vietnam three times. He was turned down, however, because he knew too much about anti-submarine warfare to be wasted in the jungle slaughter. His comment was not much different than the one I often heard thrown at dissenters when I was a kid which was, 'Why don't you go live in Russia?'

Mr. White was not angry with the boy nor was he acting in any racist capacity. But when the students in the back heard him they thought they would stir up some trouble by saying, "OOOOwwwwwwwwww he said, 'Why don't you go back to Africa?!'"

So it would seem Mr. Brown made up a story to get out of getting in trouble. All in all, I would say he had a fairly sophisticated understanding of race relations in America. He knew exactly how to get all the adults to spin like tops. After I gave my report, his mother was not satisfied and called me a racist. The Principal investigated the matter, then the Superintendent, then several members from the N.A.A.C.P. They all came to the same conclusion I did. After that the matter was put to rest.

The net result of all this was a ton of wasted instructional time, the harassment of an old man who was trying to contribute and the kid got out of his punishment. It all proved that a little dishonesty can go a long, long way.

Chapter 15

I could see he was bored. I was another flabo on his list. Another slob who's only cure would be a quart of water from the Fountain of Youth and a personalityectomy.

"Mr. Farmer," he said slowly, still focusing on the clipboard he was holding. "You have high blood pressure, high cholesterol and you're what we call pre-diabetic."

He looked up as if I'd missed my cue to speak. I said nothing, preferring to let the diagnosis rattle past in the absurd hope that if I paid no attention to it, it would go away.

"These are all diseases associated with stress. What do you do for a living?"

"I'm an assistant principal."

"Well that doesn't sound too stressful," he said, furrowing his brow in a 'Hmmm? What could it be?' way.

"It's not," I totally lied. "Probably just some bad genetics. My parents were first cousins, so you never know."

He began writing furiously on his clipboard, preferring to let my last remark go to the same place I left his diagnosis go.

I left his office without mentioning my adrenaline filled ten to fifteen hour days. Nor did I mention the nearly constant battles with no breaks. I didn't mention the stress of having to maintain a calm demeanor in the face of a parade of students and adults routinely screaming and cursing at me. And I definitely didn't mention the mountain of frustrations built up from having the jackals I work for constantly, inexplicably, sandbagging my efforts to improve the school.

I don't know why I didn't say anything. Maybe I was afraid he'd tell me I had to leave Sunnydale. For as toxic as the place was, it had gotten under my skin. Somehow I had gotten to the point where I wanted to keep pulling the lever till three of anything came up and the shiny coins tumbled out.

I didn't tell Dairy about the bad news, but she knew. She didn't like the long days and she could see the new crop of gray hair, the ever present, ever growing bags under my eyes and the weight loss.

I told myself that you can't act like bullshit is a surprise when you take a job as a bullfighter. You knew what you were doing when you signed up, so, shut up. Besides, we all get older no matter what we do.

Of course, I said it a lot nicer than that when I related my thoughts on the matter to Dairy. She wasn't buying, however. She said she didn't want to watch my destruction and she didn't want the children to watch it either.

I assured her there would be no

destruction. I got real eloquent, if not a little grandiloquent, in my speech and I managed to convince her I had it all under control. I was so good, I damned near convinced myself.

The next day the sun rose in the east and it found me ripping down the highway to Sunnydale with no thoughts or concern of my rapidly clogging circulatory system or my misfiring, misfit endocrine system, or the convenient lies my dull mind was cautiously feeding my sharp mind. I rolled on.

People soak up days like they're going to live forever. The truth is, they won't. Their bodies remember every day. Time is marked in gray hairs, wrinkles and other deformities I don't want to contemplate.

Maybe, and I can't say for sure, people spend so much time on useless, meaningless pursuits because doing so is a direct denial of their mortality. Perhaps they instinctively know something it took me a lifetime to figure out: illusion beats the hell out of reality every time.

Sunnydale ate up my time like fire eats parched forest. It remorselessly consumed very nearly my every waking hour. I can't say that I minded at first. I wanted to be a great administrator and I wasn't yet aware of how oppressive desire can be.

I'd usually fight time by combining activities or skipping them altogether, mostly lunch in the latter case. By dinner, which I usually ate while on the long drive home, I was two parts starving for every one part exhausted.

I used my little red car and a class "A" highway system to transport myself between the part of the planet that was my home and the part of the planet that was Sunnydale. I told myself it was no big deal, but it was.

My wife and children, although pleasant enough, had no comprehension of Sunnydale or poverty, or power politic for that matter. Having grown up poor, and having spent much time at Sunnydale in a ringside seat to their ruthless politics and bare-assed, unapologetic aggression, I bore witness to a world my wife and children couldn't comprehend.

That world swallowed me whole and spit me out partially digested. But I wasn't concerned about the future then. Mostly I worked on my daily diet of crisis, stress and more stress.

Dairy didn't like Sunnydale to begin with. She was uneasy about my giving up a good job near our home for an administration job so far away. And now, it seemed the cost of my working at Sunnydale, growing ever higher, had very nearly achieved a price she wasn't willing to pay.

So, I made a deal with her. I was getting good at making deals. We agreed that every Friday would be "Date Night," and no matter what, Sunnydale be damned, we'd do something together as a couple.

We sealed the deal with a kiss and I was about to make some sort of smart-ass remark about scoring on our date, but stopped myself when it occurred to me that part of this was about sex. I'm ashamed to say I had been falling behind in that department, and I'm even more ashamed to admit I thought nothing of how that affected Dairy.

Due to my genetically predetermined, disfigured condition, I, as you may have guessed, encountered a great deal of resistance from women in my formative years. Consequently, I'd developed a silly bias that women don't want sex or even like sex and come equipped with a state of the art sex avoidance system. In my defense, it's just the sort of thing an ego will do to protect itself. With my prejudice working overtime, I had assumed Dairy wouldn't be bothered when I wasn't bothering her to pay the marriage debt.

I was wrong of course and ashamed at my stupidity. In my mind, I dutifully raised my right hand in the manner of cheats, thieves, alcoholics, workaholics, creeps, freaks, gamblers and weirdoes from time immemorial, and vowed to make Date Night worth Dairy's while. And like the rest of my felonious cohort, I very nearly believed I meant it.

Chapter 16

I heard a light knock on the door. I looked up to see Rosa.

"Ayyy Sub-Rosa! What can I do for you?" She just stood there, not sure if she should answer me. It was clear something was bothering her. "Why don't you come in and sit down?"

She hesitated, then came in and took a seat.

"Is there something wrong? The reason I ask is because you don't usually stop by, especially when you're supposed to be in class."

"I know."

I could see tears forming in the corners of her eyes and I thought 'Oh shit it's a sex thing.' That is the one thing kids are always reluctant to talk about, which is understandable. Usually, every other complaint about any wrong done them is offered up with no compunction and in many instances at Sunnydale, accompanied with yelling long and loud.

"Take your time" I said and sat back giving her my full attention. "Is this something that might embarrass you telling me? If it is I can get the guidance counselor. Maybe you'd feel more comfortable telling a woman."

"No it's not that. It's just . . . Mr. Dick."

Now I was pretty sure it wasn't a sex thing but not totally sure. Mr. Dick was a loud-mouth jerk but he was an old loud-mouth jerk. I'd worked with him in every school I had ever been associated with. He was the faculty room genius who, without the benefit of actually ever having done so, always knew better how to run a school than every administrator in the world.

He started working at Sunnydale just after getting his certification in social studies thirty-five years ago. Apple told me that he'd had an affair with a student early in his career. It was said you could see his van rocking in the parking lot nearly every day after school. The student graduated and he married her. All's well that ends well?

"What's the problem with Mr. Dick?"

"He got mad at me because I didn't agree with what he was saying, then he said, we were the dumbest class he'd ever had in thirty-five years of teaching. Then he kicked me out of class."

Now I was beginning to see what had happened. Rosa, a good student and never a problem, was kicked out of class because she dared to question the teacher. Of course, I would have to confirm my suspicion before I make a final decision, but you can be damn sure she won't be getting any punishments until I straighten out the matter.

For some reason our school system likes to present knowledge and life in rigid terms. Were one to really absorb the dogma, or as Vigotsky would say 'internalize,' it, then one would walk away with absolutely no sense of nuance and a rigid belief that all matters are concrete.

Information is presented as a series of molds each containing something that has a corresponding label which, if you're smart, you'll memorize and damn well not question. Nothing angers me more than when I observe an "educator" who gets angry or pissy with a student when that student questions the doctrine.

A prime example of information treated as beyond question is spelling. Students are given a specific spelling to a group of words they are expected to memorize without question. They are, in effect, given the answers to the next test and all they need do to succeed is memorize them and put them in the order selected by the teacher on test day.

There is nothing wrong with spelling tests per se, but years and years of them combined with fat dictionaries worshiped as religious text is misleading. The spelling of words is a matter of agreement and there is no law to the universe that dictates the proper spelling of every word ever used. Most words are spelled through majority consent but not all words are spelled only one way. Words change throughout time. New words may appear and be spelled several ways before one method is generally accepted.

When I was in second grade my teacher asked us to write about what we did over our Thanksgiving holiday. I wrote about how I went to a park that had a huge rocket ship made for children to play on. It had several slides, stairways, monkey bars etc. There was one part that connected to the main rocket by a bridge of wood boards that were connected to each other by chain links so that it moved in every direction when walked upon. I described the bridge as, "a rickety rackety bridge."

My teacher handed me back my story and told me that I had to change it because "rickety" and "rackety" were not words. The paper had red marks all over it attesting to my crime of creativity, but most perplexing to my second grade mind, and my adult mind now, was the blood red "SP" under each word. I misspelled invented words? Is such a thing possible?

That teacher was, of course, a fucking idiot. But her actions indicate a firm reliance on "what is right" because that thought is based on the bedrock belief that there is a "right." It never occurred to her that words are not drop forged in heaven. All of them were invented at one time or another.

Instead of applauding my inventiveness and encouraging a discussion about conventional verses unconventional word use and perhaps an introduction of the concept of poetic license, she told me, with the blessings and the might of the entire educational system looking approvingly over her shoulder, that I was wrong.

When I became a teacher I vowed never to squelch the learning process the way she and so many of my teachers did. I never got angry with students when they questioned the system or the knowledge I was imparting to them. I never belittled their attempts to apply their artistic selves.

Labeling, like love, is an imperfect endeavor. We do it because also like love, it is natural for us. Every taxonomy is flawed. No matter how clever the system devised to name things and reduce them to a quantifiable bit of information is, it always falls short because as soon as you think you've got it down, a duck billed platypus shows up and throws it all out of whack.

Of course, I didn't tell all this to Rosa. She was a good kid and none of the aforementioned would be of any use to her now. Mr. Dick's pronouncement that they were the dumbest students he'd ever had and being kicked out of class was a bit too much for her. He had humiliated her.

That's the way it is with any class. Some students wouldn't care if you insulted them, some would put up with it, some would seethe with rage and others would cry about it. But they would all be a little less amenable to the learning process in that class afterward. Could you imagine if you went into a store to buy a pair of jeans and the salesperson starts off by telling you that you were the dumbest customer he's ever had in his thirty five years of selling jeans?

Mr. Dick was the sort of teacher who saw any student who questioned his dogma as a troublemaker. I would have liked to fire the jerk and replace him with someone less heinous but that was not an option. I would have to meet with him and probably a few of the students and probably some parents. Mr. Dick didn't know it but he'd just heaped a bunch of work on me.

I spoke with Rosa for a few moments and assured her that I would check with Mr. Dick before I meted out any punishment for being kicked out of class. I also told her that she was not stupid and that its okay to question what she was taught provided, of course, that she did so in a civil manner.

I let her stay with me for the rest of the period because if I sent her to the I.S.S. room for holding till the end of the period, she would be required to get a day in I.S.S. If I suspended the I.S.S. sentence for any reason, the woman who ran the I.S.S. would go straight to the Union rep., her sister, who would go straight to a member of the board, who would then go to the superintendent, who would then question me as to why I was soft on crime. Heaven forbid I used discretion or, dare I say it, *wisdom.*

There was an unusual focus on punishing the students at Sunnydale by the adults. They all complained that the administrators were not being fair by giving some students special treatment. The remedy for this alleged asymmetrical justice was an elaborate discipline code, which by the time everyone had put in their two cents, was longer than the U.S. Constitution.

Yet for all the rancor and abuse I and Rick suffered over this issue, Lou Mustard didn't have any problem with coming to my office to discuss the Case of the Crapper to get special treatment for his nephew. And the fact that he showed up just as Rosa was leaving to go to her next class was just another irony among so many that I hardly noticed it.

"Mr. Farmer, I gots to talk widchu," he said as he wobbled in. His tone of voice told me he was angry.

I knew what he wanted to talk about. My sharp mind was all over it. He wanted me to come up with a way to get his nephew off the hook. Perhaps, have me say I made a mistake and withdraw the charges.

There was no way I could, or would, do that. First off, the kid's confessed in front of a law enforcement officer, so saying I made a mistake wouldn't fly but it would also be unfair to the Crapper himself. Any kid who would do what he did is heading in the wrong direction. If he got out of this, the only lesson he'd walk away with is that there will always be a way out of trouble with the law. Who knows what his next caper would be? Maybe something that could get him hard time like Stubby's brothers or dead like so many other young black men.

I knew that Mustard wouldn't care about any of my concerns. I knew he was most probably not capable of understanding the complexity of the situation. But I figured I'd plow ahead and try to make him understand. What else could I do?

"Ay Lou, how you doin?"

"I'm fine," he puffed then sat down.

I sat down and said, "So what can I do for you today?"

"You can talk to me about this thing with Lafayette and why you be callin the cops on everyone."

That last part was designed to put me off kilter. Instead of focusing on what Lafayette did, we are now going to expand the conversation to include what the administrator did wrong-Abra Cadabra. Lafayette stole school property, lied to me, destroyed the work of his peers and wasted a substantial portion of my life, but that is not what is at issue. The issue has now become me and how *I* misbehaved.

"Look, I know he's your nephew but I cannot discuss this issue with you because that would be a F.E.R.P.A. violation." I could see by the look on his face he didn't know what F.E.R.P.A. is. "That's the law that protects each student's right to privacy."

"I know what it is!" he snapped. "Don't you be telling me you can't talk to me! I'm the president of the school board!"

"Actually, you're only the president of the school board when the board is in session. Other than that you are Lou Q. Public and I simply cannot discuss the matter with you."

I could see he was using all his fourteen points of I.Q. on that last one and I decided to try and reason with him. I hated the guy but I didn't think it served any purpose giving him a brain hemorrhage.

"Lou, I understand your concern. I've watched you many a time in our discipline meetings and I know you want to see this school fire on all cylinders as much as anyone," I lied. "But if you give me a moment maybe I can explain to you where I'm coming from on this in a way that doesn't compromise federal law or embarrass either of us."

"I ain't embarrassed," he said defensively.

"Perhaps I misspoke. What I meant was that you and I could discuss the matter in a way that was mutually beneficial."

He thought about it for a minute then said, "Go ahead."

I already had his game figured out. He thought that if he kept me talking he could wear me down, then after I did violate the F.E.R.P.A.

thingamajiggy I would have to give him what he wanted.

There was no way I could give him what he wanted and there was no way I was going to slip and say something that violated a student's rights, even if the kid was a pain in my ass. My game plan was to talk with him long enough to let his anger fade, then maybe reason with him. I didn't think my chances were good.

I looked at him and said, "Long ago in a galaxy far, far away."

"What?"

I repeated, "Long ago in a galaxy far, far away."

"That's that Star Wars shit ain't it?"

"Yeah, exactly. Those are great movies."

"So?"

"I'm not finished."

"Hmph."

"Ever since those movies came out people have talked about them, argued over them, wrote whole books debating the finer points of the story."

"So?"

"So the point is, it's not real. There is no Luke Skywalker, that's an actor trained to portray a character. There was no Death Star. It was all made up."

"So, don't you think I know dat?"

"Yeah Lou, and so do the people who spend all that time arguing about them. They know it's not real but that line 'Long ago in a galaxy far, far away,' lets them buy into the whole shtick. In order for school discipline to work, you have to get every person involved, students and adults, to buy into it. We don't have a clever tag line like Star Wars has and no *one* aspect of our system will go the same distance, but we can go a long way towards gaining the suspension of disbelief by treating every student the same regardless of who they are related to. Do you understand me?"

I wasn't sure he was following me. Then he said, "Yeah."

I still wasn't sure he was following me but I could see that a great deal of his anger had subsided.

"Lou, I hope you'll think about what I said and not be angry that things turned out the way they did," I said as I stood up. The stand up and walk them to the door maneuver was handy but I didn't invent it. Apple had showed it to me one day because he thought I generally gave people too much time.

I hated to do that to Lou because in as much as it's not wise to upset a Wookie, it's not wise to upset the president of the school board either. He got the hint and decided to challenge gravity one more time by pulling himself out of his chair. I walked him to the door.

He looked at me and said with a hint of belligerence, "Alright Mr. Farmer, I got you."

I think that was his way of saying, 'All right, I'm not gonna get anywhere with you now so I'll just move on.'

After he left I went back to my desk and tried to guess how long it would be before the superintendent called.

Chapter 17

Later, after I dared reason with the unreasonable Mr. Mustard, my cell phone did ring as I was on my way to the gym. It wasn't the superintendent. I knew by the ring. I had set it so that when he called my phone sounded like a British police car siren.

"Harris Farmer, the Assistant Principal who speaks truth to power. How may I help you?"

"Harris, this is Detective Sneer."

"Oh hey, did you get a chance to check out that thing I asked you about?" I was talking short hand like a mobster, because I didn't want any of the students to know what I was talking about. They had an amazing capacity to figure out what was going on with anything.

One time while working in a school long ago and far, far away, I had obtained a better job than the one I was working so I handed in my resignation. I handed it directly to the Principal, I shook his hand then went across the hall to the library. Just after I entered the librarian approached me.

"One of the students just told me you're leaving," she said.

I just stared at her while my mind did a back-flip. That was impossible. I had told no one of my intentions and I just handed in my resignation letter three minutes ago. When I recovered from the shock, I said to the librarian conspiratorially, "Yeah, but please don't tell anyone. It's a secret."

Sneer took the tack that he didn't know what I was talking about. "You mean about Ms. Siren?" he asked.

"Yeah."

"Yeah, I checked it. There is nothing to it. She hasn't done anything wrong. You don't have to worry about it."

That was great news as far as I was concerned. She was not doing weirdlies with the students and no one was the wiser. It seems I was wise to have Detective Slimeball check out the situation before I yelled fire. Another pat on the back for me.

"That's great news. Thanks."

Just then Torquisha came down the hall from the gym area.

"OOOOOhhhh Mr. Farmer you ain't supposed to be using a cell phone in school," she said as she passed me.

"Hey, you didn't see nothing!" I said, like a mobster in a cheap detective novel. She laughed and moved on.

"You can tell the Principal that I won't be filing charges on the Sanchez case. It's just his word against Apple's and this kid is always fighting."

"I'll tell him. I'm sure he'll be happy to hear that. Thanks."

"No problem. Bye."

I was in a good mood when I got down to the gym area. I was so busy recounting my good fortune that I had forgotten what reason I had for going to the gym in the first place. I stopped at the corner of the cross hall to try and recall my mission when some movement caught the corner of my eye.

It was unusual movement. There is a great deal of movement in schools all the time but something said to my subconscious that this movement was out of the ordinary. Something isn't right, it said.

I didn't move any part of my body except my eyes. I looked down the cross hall and immediately knew why my mind had tagged it as unusual. The movement was the door to the handicapped bathroom and visiting coach locker room. Since Sunnydale didn't have any wheelchair kids that bathroom/locker room was never open during school hours.

The door finished opening and Stubby stepped out. He looked both ways in a way that reminded me of a kid with a stolen laptop under his coat, then started toward the auxiliary gym at the opposite end of the hallway.

That was very curious because there were only three people that I knew of who had a key to that particular room. It's not like it was in need of high security, it's just that no one had a reason to have access to it.

Stubby hadn't seen me, probably because of the light differential between the cross hall and the main hall. I waited till he disappeared into the auxiliary gym, then I went to the handicapped bathroom door and turned the knob. It was locked. I used my key to go inside and have a look around.

There was an outsized toilet stall and sink to the left and beyond that there was an entrance way to a small room lined with lockers. A small bench was positioned in the exact center of the room.

I searched the lockers and the toilet stall. I found nothing. Nothing out of place. I stood on the bench and pressed up gently on the drop ceiling tiles in case there was something hidden there but I found nothing. There were no unusual smells or clues of any kind as to what Stubby was doing in there.

I made a mental note to talk with Apple and Rick about all this and headed back to the gym area, hoping I would remember why I was going there by the time I got there.

Chapter 18

I was in the second floor hallway just before first period when I spied Ms. Nickels inching her bulk towards her classroom. I jumped in front of her and shoved my hand out palm forward like a London traffic cop.

"Slow down Ms. Nickels! I don't want anyone to get hurt!"

She laughed then said, "Mr. Farmer, you always be funnin'."

"Well, I gotta earn my bloated salary somehow." I smiled and started to move off.

"Oh I wanted to remind you I be needin coverage next Wednesday," she said. "Cause I be goin to that T.A.P. training."

I was taken aback at this. So taken aback I actually blurted out that I had heard it was cancelled due to a lack of interest.

"I heard that training had been cancelled due to lack of interest," I said.

"No, where'd you hear dat?"

"Who knows? Mr. Farmer is not as young as he used to be. I'll make sure you're covered."

She laughed again and started towards her room. I could see she'd never make it there before the bell but then, that was a minor consideration in light of what she'd just told me.

I headed straight to Apple's office. He was on the phone so I waited quietly at the door. Perhaps that was just as well since it gave me time to cool off a little.

He hung up and I walked into the room. I closed the door but I didn't sit down.

"We need to talk."

"What about?"

"T.A.P. Training."

He smiled. The fat prick smiled like I'd just caught him cheating at solitaire.

"Yeah."

"Yeah. What do you have to tell me about it?"

"I lied to you."

"What?"

"I lied to you. I didn't want you out of the building. That would be more work for me."

"Man, that is a terrible thing to do! I never would have done that to you."

"Yeah, but what are you gonna do? Did you hear from Sneer?"

And that was it. He had no qualms about lying to me. More than that, his question about the detective was his way of telling me he didn't want to discuss the matter further.

I punished kids five days a week and I often gave them a short sermon on having to take responsibility for their actions. If I thought the guy who was in charge of their school was capable of understanding any of it I might have given the sermon to him at this moment.

That was the thing that always got me about the adults in schools. They constantly carped about the kids doing the very things they themselves did. If a student lied and mistreated a colleague, that would be wrong, but when the Principal does it, it's charming?

"Yes, I did speak with him," I said. "He said they are not going to file charges on that Sanchez thing."

"Good."

"I bet the kid's stepdad is going to be pissed."

"The hell with him. He's nuts anyway. That little bastard deserved to be smashed into that door."

"You mean you did smash him up against the door jamb?"

"Hell yeah! He was being a jerk."

I couldn't believe this guy. Any more lies and evil behavior and he's going to skip assistant superintendent and go right to the top slot.

"You told me that he fell," I reminded him, although I don't know why.

"I lied," he said turning back to his computer.

"That kid has cerebral palsy. You could have injured him badly."

"What? He's fine. That's not gonna hurt a kid like that."

I had to get out of there. This guy was making me sick. I should have wanted to slam him up against a door jamb but my contempt for him was beyond even that. Besides, I doubt there is anything I could do to persuade him that brutalizing students is a bad thing.

I got to the door then turned back, "By the way, Sneer says that Rick and I were wrong about the Ms. Siren thing."

"Good," he said, turning his attention from his computer screen to the paper work on his desk.

I walked out of there mad as hell and I think he knew it. Of course he didn't care one bit. Apple was the sort of person who had no sense of what I call 'problem permanence.' If a problem didn't affect him, it didn't exist. For him, our country was not involved in Vietnam until the day the draft system was changed and it was possible that he might have to go.

As a sonofabitch, he easily found a way out of military service but once his ass was over the fence, he supported military action in just about any defenseless third world nation you could name.

I had been cheated and lied to and there simply was no recourse. If the teachers were mistreated as I had been they could run to their union, if the students were upset they could run to their parents, who either went to the board or the superintendent, but there was nowhere for me to go. I had to eat it, and it didn't taste good.

Chapter 19

After my meeting with Apple, principal liar, I decided that I couldn't go to dinner with Dairy. After so many years of marriage she was well acquainted with my dark side but I couldn't subject her to the mood I was in.

I went out to a spot in the lobby that was far away from any ears and I called Dairy.

"Hello?"

"Hey, it's me."

"Who?" she asked.

"Don't toy with me. I am very jealous and I have low self esteem."

"Oh that sounds like a winning combination," she said in a voice that made me believe she was smiling.

"Listen, I can't make it tonight. I'm real sorry."

"Why not?"

I paused. Damn, I hadn't prepared a statement. Or more to the point, I didn't have a lie prepared because I was in a bad mood because I had been lied to. It was a chain reaction of prevarication that I was to find out later wasn't quite at critical mass but would become so. Nevertheless, I had to say something. What was I supposed to say? *'I have to break our date because I'm a fucked up mess?'*

"I'd rather not say but if you forgive me for this I'll forgive you for seducing me on our last date."

"Ohhhhh, I seduced you!?"

I knew that would get her.

"You know it."

"Okay Farmer, I gotta go. Someone is on the other line. I'll let you off the hook this time but you'd better make it up to me."

"Yes, I will. Thanks, bye."

"Bye."

I hung up and decided to take a walk down to the woodshop and see how Woods was doing. He'd been in my office yesterday screaming up a storm because one or more of the students filled his desk drawers to the brim with shaving cream.

I told him that I would catch the culprits and bring them to justice. I didn't tell him that I wasn't sure if that meant punishing them or rewarding them.

Still, he was lucky in that it was shaving cream. Apple told me once that several years before I was hired there was an English teacher who was quite nuts and much disliked by the students. One of them decided to get back at her by having a bowel movement in one of her desk drawers. She had worked there so long and was so sure of where everything was that she didn't look into the drawer, she just pulled it open and reached in to get something. He said people three towns over from Sunnydale heard her scream.

Just as I was rounding the corner to the main hallway I saw Torquisha standing by the girls' gang lavatory door. She was just standing there staring off into space.

"Torki! You're standing there doing nothing like you're some sort of school administrator. Whatsup?"

"Mr. Farmer aw . . . I be in trouble."

There's only one response to that statement.

"Let's go to my office."

She nodded and we both started for my office. We didn't speak the whole way. Torquisha started to cry the moment we stepped inside my office. We sat down and I handed her a tissue. I waited patiently for her to talk.

"Mr. Farmer I be in trouble. My momma gonna kill me."

"Torquisha, when you say 'trouble' I take it you mean pregnant?"

"Yeah."

"I don't know what to do. What should I do?"

"Torquisha, nobody in this institution likes you more than I do but I cannot help you. At least not in the way you want me to. You've made some adult decisions and now you have to deal with some adult consequences."

She thought about that for a moment. The whole situation hit her and the emotions welled up. "Being an adult sucks!" she cried.

"It seemed a whole lot better in the brochure, I'll admit."

"I don't know what to do... Please don't tell anyone. I didn't even be telling Stubby."

Oh shit. I didn't like the sound of that.

"What does he have to do with this?" I asked, hoping beyond hope that she wouldn't answer the way I thought she would.

"He be the father."

And there it was. *That sonofabitch!* I'll bet that day I caught him coming out of the handicapped bathroom he was in there having a tryst with this kid. That's where she was coming from when she passed me as I was talking to Detective Sneer on the phone.

"Not that it's any of my business, have you decided when and how you are going to tell your mother about this?"

"Nah, she gonna kill me. For real yo."

I didn't doubt that. Torquisha looked like a copy of her mother, albeit a smaller version with a smaller hairdo, but her mom was a mean, tough woman.

But I felt sorry for Torquisha. This girl was not a slut, she was a victim. The dirty little secret about teenage pregnancy in America is that most of the time, the girl is impregnated by a male substantially older than herself.

"I doubt she'll do that," I said trying to reassure her. "What do you say we wait a few minutes then we give Mom a call?"

Chapter 20

Calling Torquisha's mother was one of the hardest things I ever had to do as a school administrator. We called her and she blew a fuse. After I informed the Superintendent, the Principal and the School Board, they blew a fuse. When the story hit the paper, the District Attorney blew a fuse. He started a grand jury investigation of Sunnydale.

As if Stubby, an employee of the district impregnating a student wasn't bad enough, it turns out Stubby was a convicted felon. His being hired to work in a school with his record was illegal.

In a way, I couldn't blame the District Attorney for investigating Sunnydale, considering what had happened, but I was concerned. Not just because I was one of the people being investigated, but because the basic mission of any school is to increase learning and all my experience in education has made me aware of the simple fact that once lawyers get involved: *nobody learns nothin'*.

Before we could fire Stubby however, he was arrested. When the police pulled him over for a traffic violation they found a large quantity of drugs in his van, apparently ready for sale in hundreds of little baggies. I guess I should be grateful that one astute cop saved me the trouble of strangling Stubby.

We had entered dark times at Sunnydale. I could tell that the whole deal really hurt the students. They always acted tough and uncaring but, underneath all that media induced bravado, I could see they were having a hard time of it. They were confused and wanted to make sense of it.

The school board said nothing. The principal and the superintendent refused to step up to the plate. Rick and I were left to deal with it. We had considered having a school assembly but then thought that could lead to disaster on several levels, not the least of which was a total lack of cooperation by the teachers towards that end.

In the end, we opted to speak with the students in the classrooms in a less formal way. I took grades seven through nine. I didn't walk in and say, "I'm here to discuss the Stubby situation." I would walk into each classroom as if I were just saying hi, then invariably one student would ask about Stubby.

"Hey Mr. Farmer, what's happening with Stubby?"

I would reply, "Well, Mr. Stubby won't be working here anymore."

"Cause he got arrested?"

"Yeah, why'd he do dat Mr. Farmer?"

"I don't know what motivated Mr. Stubby to do what he did. The truth is, people don't always behave in ways that you want them to. They sometimes act in ways which hurt other people. That's one of the reasons we spend so much time in this school trying to teach everyone how to behave properly. And as tragic as all this is, I suppose if we learn from it and somehow use that knowledge to lead better lives and don't make the mistakes Mr. Stubby made, then maybe some good can come from all of this."

"You think he be going to jail?"

"Well, he's in jail now but more than that I cannot say. I'm just an outrageously good looking school administrator, not a lawyer."

Then they would laugh and I would tell a few more jokes or talk it out some more depending on the feel of it. After a while, when I thought no more could be gained from the session, I'd act like I just realized I was intruding on the teacher's class.

"Oh hey, listen to me talking like crazy over here when Mrs, or Mr. So-and-So wants to teach you something." Then the class would groan because anybody who isn't the teacher making them work is a welcomed speaker. I'd smile, make my exit then go to the next class.

It was the same routine all over the school but I'm not sure how much it helped. I noticed that the misbehaviors increased and attendance, which was never real great at Sunnydale, slipped big time. I tried to get out more and spend more time with the students putting the paperwork off till after school, which meant more and more late nights. It also meant I had to cancel a few more dates with Dairy, which really hurt.

Sadly, the dark times at Sunnydale got darker and one of the reasons for that was because I didn't cancel a date with Dairy.

I don't recall what we were supposed to be doing on our date, but around five in the afternoon I still had a ton of paperwork to get through, and several parents I had to call back, and some good-will calls.

Good-will calls were what I called parent contacts wherein I said nice things about their kids. I figured if I am quick to call when a student does something bad, why shouldn't I call if they do well? Fair is fair. Ironically, there were some parents who had become so used to getting bad calls about their kids that they just didn't know how to take good-will calls.

My first semester as a teacher I was so gung-ho that I sent home a progress report with every student. The next day one of my students told me he'd gotten a "lickin'." That particular school was the complete opposite of Sunnydale, it was rural, and whiter than mayo on Wonder Bread.

At first I didn't know what he meant, especially because I had sent a good report home on him. His parents never bothered to open it. They saw who it was from and they just knew it contained information on some form of negative behavior by their son. They put the unopened envelope down on the television and beat the hell out of the kid.

After that I decided to make phone calls instead of sending mailers. I was thinking about that and how I should cancel with Dairy because I didn't want the work to build up to where I would start forgetting things. But I decided that she had been patient enough and as much as I cared for her, I wasn't sure how she was feeling about me as of late. One more stupid move by me and she might decide to cut her losses.

I'll admit that the idea of Date Night with my wife seemed much better when I was drunk. But lately, even sober the idea had its charms.

And Dairy was a good wife. She was compassionate, honest, intelligent, a snappy dresser when she wanted to be and not hard on the eyes.

On our wedding day I figured that eventually she was going to figure out what a freak I was and consequently, the marriage would only last so long. The marriage lasted way longer than I thought it would. For all her brains and talents, Dairy never seemed to figure out how much better she was than me.

I started to think about the first time I saw her totally nude. That sealed the deal. I was not going to cancel our date. I just wished I could remember what we were supposed to be doing.

I hit the speed dial.

"Hello?" she said.

"Ay, It's your reason for living."

"You're calling to cancel aren't you?" she asked knowingly.

"Not as such, no. I wanted to cancel our plans and substitute other plans."

"What's the substitution?" she asked, now sounding suspicious.

"I want you to meet me in that town that's halfway between the house and Sunnydale and we go see a movie there."

She said nothing, but that didn't mean she was mad. Dairy often took her time talking, as opposed to me who felt I had to respond to people like I was serving burgers in a fast food restaurant. She was very comfortable with herself, a trait that is easier to come by when you look as good as she does.

Nevertheless, I admired her for her guile deficit. Working night and day at Sunnydale where bullshit grew out of the walls, she was refreshing to be around.

"Okay," was all she said.

I wasn't sure if it was a good okay or a bad okay but, in the end, I considered it a win since I didn't cancel and neither did she.

We met in front of the theater about fifteen minutes before it was scheduled to open. She had on a pair of jeans, a button down shirt with the first two buttons undone and a buff leather jacket that followed her form like shrink wrap. She was hot.

"Wow," was all I could say. I was staring.

"You like?"

"Dairy, I like very much. You look almost as good as me."

She laughed at that because she could read what I was really thinking by looking at the way I was looking at her. She had seen many men look at her that way.

I was damned glad to see her but my mind still wasn't quite transitioned between the world of Sunnydale and the world of my domesticity. I usually had nearly two hours for that on my Friday night drive home. We stood in silence.

"What's wrong?" Dairy asked, which kind of annoyed me because I knew she was asking only because I wasn't saying anything. She did that. It's true I'm a talker but Dairy's question, was to me like saying, 'You're such a friggin blowhard that if you're not talkin something must be wrong!'

I decided to ignore my feelings of insult and jump into a conversation to pass the time. I said, "Nothing. I was just thinking about an idea for a movie." I nodded to the nearby movie poster in a small glass case sunk into the front wall of the theater. She looked at it and I snuck a quick look at her cleavage, which looked magnificent.

"Well, don't keep me waiting. Let's have it," she said, turning back to me with her eyes sparkling, reminding me of the first time I met her. I dove in.

"What about a movie about a small high school in a remote area, an area so remote that the school board cannot attract a suitable candidate for principal so they purchase a robot principal? The robot principal is knowledgeable and fair however, he has the unfortunate habit of vaporizing a recalcitrant student or two from time to time with laser bolts from his optical units. Of course this upsets the school board but they cannot fire him due to a little known codicil in the tenure laws which specifically state that artificial school officials cannot be fired if they use original equipment while dispensing discipline."

"So what does the school board do?" she asked.

"Well, naturally, the students are worried and work diligently to correct the problem," I said. "After much discussion, and a small massacre following a food fight in the cafeteria, they hit upon the idea of building a robot wife and a robot son for the robot principal. The students quickly realize that in order for their plan to work they are going to have to hit the books. Meanwhile, changes in the state legislature initiate school reform. The frustrated school board seizes the opportunity to fire the robot principal just as the students complete their task. The robot principal is glad to have a robot wife and robot son but he is saddened he has lost the job he loves."

"Is that it?" she asked.

"No, there's more. You wanna hear it?" I asked, even though I knew she loved this whole bit. I stuck in the part about the principal getting happy after getting a wife as a subliminal message. It was stupid I know, but when you have all the charm of broken glass in ice cream and you're trying to keep your better than average wife, you have to employ some unconventional methods.

"During a tearful farewell to the robot principal and his newly manufactured family, the students and faculty realize that in their drive to improve their school, they, in fact, improved themselves. In an ironic twist they decide to embrace the robot principal and literally carry him to where the school board is meeting and demand that he be reinstated. They make an impassioned argument for the robot principal. The school board refuses and it would seem all is lost."

"Now I definitely want to know what happens next," she said, smiling broadly.

"I don't know, maybe you should just wait till the movie comes out. I don't want to ruin it for you."

"No tell me," she pleaded in a voice that was so little girl sexy my heart rate increased. After that there was no way I was not going to finish the story, even though I really hadn't thought of an ending.

"Okay. For you," I said, as if I were doing so as a favor. "Just as the cause is seemingly lost, the robot principal determines that the school board acted improperly when they failed to adhere to the wishes of the people who voted for them and vaporizes the entire board with laser bolts from his optical units. A new board is appointed and the robot principal is reinstated. And aside from the occasional vaporization of a foreign exchange student, they all live happily ever after and the high school becomes the M.I.T. of rural schools."

"What is the point of the story?" she asked.

"I suppose the point is that schools are communities and it is all the parts of the community that determine the effectiveness of the school," I said. "Plus a school board gets vaporized, I liked that part."

"Yeah?"

"Yeah. You constantly hear people go on and on about what's wrong with the schools and then offer a cure, which is usually based on altering one aspect, like getting rid of tenure, or firing the administrators or having school prayer."

"So you're saying that you can't know how to fix the schools if you don't see them as a community?"

"I guess what I'm saying is that if you want to improve any school, and certainly there are some more dysfunctional than others, you have to take a holistic approach to the school community. It doesn't matter if you hire a principal with the efficiency of a robot, if the parents neglect their kids, or if the school has terrible teachers, or if the school board is corrupt and non responsive to the needs of the community."

Jesus, now I was giving a speech. I should have said the point of the story with the robot was to make her laugh. Now she thinks I'm an egghead. I had been assigned that moniker from time to time throughout my life.

I thought that academia was the one place I didn't have to hide my smarts, but I was mistaken. One day the people in the State Education Department decided that one of the ways they could look as if they were doing their jobs would be to have all the teachers take the test developed for the eleventh graders in Math and English. After the waste of time was completed I was in the teachers' lounge when one of the math teachers asked me how I had done. I told her that I had gotten a perfect score.

I told her my score without pride because I had assumed that all the teachers had gotten a perfect score. I mean it was a test for eleventh graders, right? What I didn't know was that I was the only teacher to get perfect scores in both parts of the test and the others resented it.

Dairy didn't say anything for a moment, as if she was mulling it over, which she probably was, but I didn't want to talk about it anymore. The whole conundrum was giving me a headache. I decided to talk about her work for a change.

"So how'd things go down at the zoo today?"

"Oh not bad, several of the monkeys tried to bust my chops but nothing unusual. Are you saying that because schools are so complex they can't be improved?"

Dairy didn't give up easily, which is a great trait for the mother of your children to have but I'm not so sure I like it in a wife.

"No, I was just saying that school reform should be done comprehensively. How'd the monkeys do it?"

"Do what? Oh, bust my chops."

I had finally managed to change the topic but to be honest, for the rest of it, I was back at Sunnydale. I could hear her voice changing in volume while she talked but I didn't really pay attention. I was pretty sure I didn't have to. I also got a couple more surreptitious glances at her beckoning breasts while she concentrated on her tale of woe.

"Wow, that's some smart monkeys," I said, when I was pretty sure she was near to putting on the capstone to her story.

"Well they're just doing what primates do, I suppose. I put a stop to it."

I had always wondered about how someone like Dairy, an avowed people lover, could justify some of the things she did in her disputes with others. I never asked her, however. I knew that in the end, her answer would be some version of the old standard rationalization that we do bad things because it leads to a greater good. I'd been getting by on that one as an educator for years.

Still, I could see the similarity between her coworkers and the students. They were placed in unnatural situations that they wanted out of.

I decided to place those thoughts in the I'll-get-to-it-later pile because just then a pimply-faced employee unlocked the front door.

"Shall we go?" she asked.

We stepped inside, bought our tickets and proceeded into the theater taking our seats. We were alone in the semidarkness.

"Hey hon," I whispered.

"What?" she whispered back.

"You wanta do me a favor?" I whispered and started giggling.

"Keep it in your pants loverboy," she whispered sternly.

Then a theatergoer walked in and took a seat. He was followed by others. The theater filled up quickly after that. The previews started and I suddenly got real hungry. I told Dairy I was going for some theater grub and I'd be back before the start of the film.

I returned in record time and just as I was taking my seat I saw something so strongly with my sharp mind, my dull mind didn't have a chance in hell of stopping it.

"Holy shit!" I blurted out.

"What?" Dairy said, stiffening as if we were about to have a car crash.

"I don't believe it. Sonofa-,"

"What?" Dairy whispered, "Keep your voice down!"

"Listen I'm gonna take you home I gotta take care of something."

"What?"

"I'm sorry but it's something I have to do. I-,"

"Does this have to do with work?"

"C'mon," I said, grabbing her by the sleeve almost yanking her out of the seat.

I was pretty sure of what I'd just seen and I damn well didn't want Dairy in that theater. I knew she'd be pissed but there was nothing I could do about that. I hustled her out of the theater and all the way to her car. She was so mad I could feel the heat coming off of her. She started to work the seatbelt buckle the instant she was behind the wheel.

"Dairy I'll be home soon after you and explain."

"Save it!" she said without looking at me.

She got the car started, slammed it in gear and drove off. I hated to do it but I had to check out the scene and I couldn't involve Dairy in that. My mind was spinning when she pulled away but I did make a mental note to call her as soon as was possible.

I don't know what the hell I was thinking when I headed back to the movie theater. Between the teachers, my administrator 'colleagues,' the school board, Stubby and the Grand Jury investigation, this whole school administrator bit was beginning to give off a creepy Heart of Darkness vibe. I should have seen that as a warning and turned back but instead I kept moving up river.

I didn't have a disguise but the movie had already started and I was pretty sure I could slip in unnoticed. The trick was going to be finding them in the dark.

I bought one of those garbage can sized buckets of popcorn and a soda to hide behind and headed for the dark.

The theater was wide with a center aisle and an aisle on each side along the wall. I took a position in the right rear of the movie theater so I had a diagonal view of most of the patrons. I started a slow scan with my eyes only.

I did not feel right about any of this. Spying on an employee was wrong. Moreover, I wasn't sure if what I was doing was illegal. Certainly, it was not covered in principal school.

There was a great many things about being a school administrator not covered in administration school, criminal justice being top on the list. Over the past eight months I had to investigate, weigh evidence and pass sentence numerous times. I had to listen to witness testimony and decide what was valid and what was not. I spent a great deal of my time on non educational stuff.

When I started out I had visions of me helping teachers, guiding students, handing out awards, instead I wound up in the back of a movie theater spying on a possible child molester. I had gotten so far from where I thought I'd be that I was ashamed of myself.

Yet, through all these thoughts I continued to scan the crowd. My years of cafeteria management paid off because I picked her out of the crowd in record time. She had her hair twisted on her right side behind her ear and I got a good view of her face. It was her alright, Ms. Siren. I couldn't see the person to her right because there was someone else's head in the way but I was pretty sure I wasn't going to like it.

After Detective Sneer told us she was not involved with students inappropriately, Rick and I decided to have a talk with her about the matter. We weren't going to tell her about us having her investigated but we were going to warn her to avoid the appearance of impropriety. Luckily, I was unavailable for that meeting because if I had lectured her on the appearance of impropriety I would feel twice as bad as I did now about spying on her.

She moved close to her partner and I thought for a minute she was going to kiss him, but she just was making some sort of comment to her date. Then the movie had a daylight scene and everything was much more visible in the audience so I slumped down in my chair.

I noticed someone had just entered the theater on the other side. I didn't think much of it but then another daylight scene came on the screen and I could see it was Dairy! I slumped down further in my chair hoping I could figure a way out. I also made a mental note to thank God later for having her pick the wrong side of the theater to start searching for me.

She was mad as hell at me and when she started the drive home thinking about what had happened, she got even madder. She'd guessed I was going to go back into the theater and decided to go back to the theater and give me a piece of her mind.

I wasn't entirely sure what Dairy would do there if she found me but I was certain I didn't want to find out. I slid out of my chair and crawled along the seats to the aisle along the wall, then headed toward the exit. I saw her, still on the other side of the theater, moving toward the back of the theater as I was. I immediately reversed course. I started toward the front of the theater hoping an opportunity to disappear would show up.

She was super pissed and diligently looking for me. I should have been annoyed that she was putting me in an awkward situation, but I had to admit I felt a little pride in her for being so smart and strong, as I literally crawled away from her and my dignity.

My sharp mind and my dull mind were clashing furiously in my head. If Dairy found me she'd probably give me the business and my surveillance would be blown. If she caught me crawling on the floor she'd probably dump me for being a jerk and if I explained everything to her she'd probably dump me for being an idiot. In any case, it was not good, so I continued to crawl.

Dairy walked along the back of the theater and headed over towards my side. Once she got to the head of the aisle I was caught. She was part blood hound or something. My heart really started pounding and my brain was absolutely no help. Just as she approached the aisle, my autonomic nervous system kicked in and I dove into a row.

I suppressed my gag reflex at the filthy, sticky, slimy floor and pressed myself into the underside of the seats. I couldn't see or hear her but I sensed she was walking slowly down the aisle, carefully checking each row. My only hope lay in her not seeing my prostrate form.

I read about these pirates once who, when their ship was dismasted by a British Man-of-War, simply stopped firing, went below and started drinking heavily. They knew the instant that mast came crashing down on the deck that all hope of victory or escape was finished. Lying in the sticky ooze beneath the seats, I knew exactly how they must have felt. I was about to get caught in a very embarrassing situation and there was nothing I could do about it.

I waited and nothing happened. By my calculations she should have been here stomping my guts out by now. It occurred to me that she'd left. I could be home free, but giving in to my searing desire to jump up off that nauseating morass on the floor would be a mistake. I had to make sure the coast was clear.

I started to crawl through the muck towards the center aisle. I figured if I got far enough away from Dairy's last known location I could sneak a peek and not get caught. There were lumpy things, sticky things, and smelly things throughout my route and I crawled through them all. Cowardice does indeed have a high price. I was gagging the whole way.

I got three seats from the center aisle and decided to chance a look. I couldn't believe it, but Dairy had stopped at the row just before mine.

Something on the screen had caught her eye and she was watching the movie. I came within seconds of being caught, but then my situation hadn't improved all that much. If she continued her search and there was a concomitant daylight scene she might still catch me.

I figured as soon as whatever it was that had her attention let it go, she would resume her search and I didn't want that so I slipped my cell phone out and hid its light by holding it underneath me and hit the speed dial. I figured she was so pissed and in such a hurry that she didn't turn off the ringer as theater protocol directed. I only hoped that she wasn't in so much of a hurry that she forgot to bring it with her.

I heard the bum, bum bum da bum bum bum bum of her Mozart ringtone and I stiffened in anticipation. I sure as hell couldn't talk to her but I was hoping she'd go outside to answer it.

Several people made noises of derision and one person yelled out, "Take it outside honey!"

I heard the bum, bum bum da bum bum bum bum a second time and I could tell it was moving away from me. I knew then my ruse had worked, but I still had to get out of there fast because as soon as she got outside and realized there was no one on the line, she was likely to come back.

I pulled myself off the floor, gagging one more time for luck, then headed for the men's room. I went up to the door Dairy had originally come in through. I looked through the little square window in its center to see if she was still prowling for me. She was there in the lobby stabbing at the keys of her cell phone with her right forefinger and frowning. Great with people, lousy with technology. I decided to wait her out.

I guess it was my years as a cafeteria slave that caused me to check the theater behind me. I stone froze because Ms. Siren and her "date" were coming up the aisle with their arms wrapped around each other.

I was milliseconds away from getting caught by both parties. There was no way out this time. If there was a solution, I figured it was so complicated, there simply wasn't enough time to figure it out.

I checked back at Dairy and she was just closing up her phone and hooking it back on one of her beautiful hips which I would most probably never be permitted to touch again. I glanced back to see Ms. Siren and Co. were almost at the top of the aisle. In another five seconds they would make the turn and be face-to-face with me.

I damn near panicked, but then my sharp mind kicked in and provided me with a simple plan that was just stupid enough to work. I turned with my back toward them and started away, then knelt down and started tying my shoe. I could hear the door open behind me and I saw Ms. Siren's right hand glide past the very edge of my peripheral vision.

I heard her say "Thank you," then I heard Dairy say "You're welcome." They were three feet behind me and my imaginary, stubborn shoelace. Dairy was holding the door for them.

I didn't dare look up when I heard the door close but I heard Dairy walk right past me. She must have been searching the crowd and looked right over me. I waited a beat after she passed me, then I turned away from where she was as I rose to leave the theater.

Just as I entered the lobby I saw Ms. Siren exiting the front doors. She and her date, who I could now see clearly under the marquee lights was one of our students, stopped. They turned to each other and started a heavy duty kiss that made them look like they were trying to swallow one another.

I walked towards the door, took out my cell phone and snapped pictures till I got as close as I dared then veered off toward the men's room. They finished their kiss, oblivious to me or my handy phone cam, and set off for Ms. Siren's car.

I had thought about confronting her then and there and stopping them from doing what I think they left the movie early to do, but then, I was covered in filth and I had Dairy still searching for me. I chose to make a clean getaway.

The next day I went to Apple with the photos and as much of the story as I dared tell. We both went down to the Generalissimo, Dr. Mayonnaise. I insisted on going because I didn't want Apple to take credit for my work, but I also didn't trust him to say what needed to be said.

Even Dr. Mayonnaise had to agree with me that she needed to be fired. There was no other way, but I knew he would do what he could to get out of it. He could see that I was adamant about it. What I couldn't see was, why he wasn't.

It was obvious to me that the great Detective Sneer dropped the ball and it was equally obvious that after Rick had his little heart-to-heart discussion with Ms. Siren she chose to view it as a sign she should take better care to hide her illicit activities, e.g. go on a date two towns over, rather than end her activities altogether. She was a fucking idiot who not only deserved to be fired, but should have gotten a swift kick in the ass on the way out the door.

Later that day, Rick, Apple and Brannon the computer guy went up to her classroom during her planning period. She was asked for her computer password and Brannon took her out of the system right then and there.

She didn't say a word when they fired her, although curiously, she had a slight smile on her face.

Chapter 21

In the weeks following Stubby's arrest and Ms. Siren's firing, the Grand Jury Investigation picked up steam. Everyone was called in to testify. I was spared because Stubby had been hired before I was so I had nothing to do with it. However, it was made clear to me by slithering Detective Sneer that I was being investigated. Clearly a crime had been committed in the hiring of Stubby. The D.A. smelled blood and he figured he would keep circling swimmers till one of them was ready for a bite.

A curious thing started to happen concerning Stubby and Ms. Siren, everyone started talking. The veil of secrecy had been broken. I was stunned at this because I didn't think the people at Sunnydale were capable of keeping any thoughts to themselves. The worst blabbermouth of them all was Assistant Superintendent Dirt. I think the reason he was incapable of keeping a secret was because he didn't have the brain power to understand the concept. I never held it against him because you can't blame a doorknob for being a doorknob.

It seemed everyone in the loop, and a surprising number outside the loop, knew that Stubby had been in prison before. He had been arrested for selling drugs and beating some woman over a dispute about welfare money several years before he showed up at Sunnydale. Another woman had an order of protection against him for reasons unknown.

One of the Spanish teachers told me that her friend had gone to high school with Ms. Siren and said that Ms. Siren had slept with nearly every guy in her high school.

One of the local police had come to the office to get my signature on several papers. While I was signing the numerous forms, he said,

"Yeah, I saw in the paper you had trouble with your hall monitor."

"Yeah, he's going to take a rather long leave of absence I think," I said, not really getting behind the joke.

The cop must have sensed my mood because he dropped his smile and said, "You know, we were all wondering how he got his job here in the first place. Don't you have to have criminal clearance to work in a school?"

"You do, but this state only requires a state criminal background check. Stubby was arrested for Federal crimes. As far as his state criminal background check was concerned, he had no record."

Wait a minute!

"You guys knew he had been arrested before?" I asked.

"Oh yeah, everybody in the department knew. Stubby played football for Spartanburg High. He was a helluva runner. He got a scholarship to a school I believe was in Ohio. But he quit his first year."

"Penn State"

"Oh yeah, Penn State."

So the police _knew_ this guy was a criminal working in the local school but said nothing. Now the DA was acting all outraged that this could happen and it seems it was a widely kept secret in his own Police Department. As it turned out, the police were not the only ones.

After the policeman left my office, my sharp mind went to work. It went to a memory I have of an English teacher and a Business teacher I once worked with. They were both married and obviously having a thing. Every teacher in the place was convinced of their affair, but my dull mind absolutely forbade me to accept such gossip so I refused to believe. But these two alleged adulterers were so obvious and blatant in their behaviors that even my dull mind had to concede there was something untoward going on between them.

Accepting the fact that they were indeed doing the dirty deed led me to a bit of a conundrum. Why would two people who were supposed to be doing something clandestine leave a trail a drunken monkey could follow? Why did they take no precaution to hide their secret? I thought about it long and hard until the solution hit me, it was the most unlikely and the most obvious: They didn't bother to hide their affair from their spouses because their spouses already knew about it and approved. It was very possible they were engaging in spouse swapping.

It took my sharp mind some time to convince my dull mind to accept this truth because it is so far from something I would do, that it is hard for me to accept that anyone would do it but hey, lots of people play Bingo too.

I guess I was thinking back to the English teacher and the Business teacher doing business because it was analogous to the Stubby situation. The local police said nothing because they knew that the people who ran the school, i.e. the school board and the administrators, all knew about Stubby's past and hired him anyway.

I headed over to Apple's office to confirm my suspicions. He was parked behind his computer, of course. I closed the door and sat down. I was about to say, "We need to talk," when he said without looking up from his computer, "I was just going to call you."

He took a moment to finish what he was doing. In that moment I noticed that the pattern on his sport coat wasn't a pattern at all, but rather it was a billion pills protruding from the frayed garment. I wouldn't put that coat on a garage floor for fear of dirtying-up the floor and this guy was wearing it.

"Detective Sneer came by."

"Did you count the silverware?"

"He says the DA believes Lou Mustard knew about Stubby and he wants me to wear a wire."

I didn't expect him to say that. This was getting out of hand. I started to say that but I caught myself. It occurred to me that he may already have a wire on him. Now these guys were making *me* paranoid.

The DA was getting angry and desperate. Somehow Lou and the Superintendent had managed to cover their tracks. When the DA asked Lou under oath if he knew that Stubby was a criminal when hired, Lou said no. The DA knew that Lou had lied. All he needed was a witness to corroborate it and Lou was as good as bagged.

I think that when the DA couldn't find even one person to come forward, he started to seek other means of bringing Lou down. Wiring Apple was one of his ideas to get Lou. The plan was for Apple to engage Lou in conversation then get him to say something incriminating.

I was surprised to hear all this but I was also a little suspicious. Apple was a talker but I never got the impression he considered me a confidante. So why was he telling me this now?

I said something noncommittal hoping he wouldn't ask me outright what I thought he should do. He almost never asked me what he should do on any matter so I was pretty sure he was just blowing off a little steam.

Then he asked, "Whataya think I should do?"

I felt the adrenaline stab my stomach. Now I had to answer with something and I wasn't sure if it was going on the record via a bug on this guy, which he could have easily kept hidden on the outside of his coat among the abundant pills and pulls.

If Apple did have a wire on him, it wouldn't be the first time. A few years after Apple barely managed to get a college degree his father, an accountant to some of the wealthiest businessmen in the state, hooked him up with a man who owned a number of fast food places.

The restaurant owner believed one of his managers was skimming the take so he asked Apple to investigate the guy for him. The manager in question was so adept at falsifying the records no one could catch him at it.

The plan was for Apple to gain the man's confidence then get him to confess on tape. Apple followed the guy to a bar and struck up a conversation with him. He hung around the guy for almost three weeks. They did everything together and I believe Apple even took the guy's sister on a date. As soon as he thought the time was ripe Apple steered the conversation, over some beers, to the concept of getting away with something.

The guy fell right into the trap. He started blabbing and giving all sorts of details. Apple kept refilling his beer and asking questions, letting this guy dig his own grave deeper.

The worst part of the whole story, which Apple had told me several times, was that the guy was hurt that Apple wasn't really his friend and that they wouldn't see each other after he got out of prison. That was the part Apple relished most. When he got to how the guy said slowly, "So you're not really my friend?" Apple would laugh like a drunken pirate sitting on a treasure chest.

I knew that Apple would have no problem wearing a wire and no problem using it to strangle my career. I said, real careful and slightly slower than I normally speak so there wouldn't be any distortion on any possible recording device, "I am not a lawyer and I cannot offer any useful advice on the subject. I'm sorry, but it's just not my area."

If Apple was hip to what I was thinking he didn't let on. He launched into describing a conversation he'd had with Lou, sans a wire according to him, about the Grand Jury investigation. As two who had testified, it was illegal for them to discuss what went on during their time there. They did anyway and now he was telling me what had happened.

I was uncomfortable with this because technically, we were breaking the law. I was also fascinated at how much Lou knew of what was going on in the Grand Jury. He had a mole on the jury. If the DA knew that he would have hit the ceiling.

Why Lou would take Apple into his confidence that way is anybody's guess. I think it's because Lou knew, as I did, that Apple was a palliative principal. Apple had no intention, nor the ability, to improve the school in any way and he would never stick his neck out for anyone, let alone the students he was charged with educating.

That Apple had a subtle contempt for the students at Sunnydale wasn't surprising to me. He was born to very comfortable circumstances. Lou however, was from Sunnydale and he had been one of a half-dozen children his parents couldn't afford. His hatred of the poor was as inexplicable as it was unforgivable.

Lou didn't necessarily hate black people, he hated poor blacks. On several occasions he made known his dislike for the people of the Section Eight housing program run by the federal government. For many of our students the Section Eight program was the only thing that kept them from homelessness.

Having grown up in a white version of Sunnydale's Section Eight housing program, I held no negative emotions towards the people who came from there. That fact in itself made Apple suspicious of me. I, of course, had better reasons than his attitude towards the less fortunate to be suspicious of him.

If even half of what Apple was telling me was accurate, then I would say the DA was going to have a hell of a time getting Lou dead-to-rights guilty. Assuming the DA was looking to actually solve the case, as opposed to just using it for some publicity points. I wasn't sure what the DA's intention was because he didn't seem to be swinging for the fences and he was in the paper nearly every day with comments about what was supposed to be a sealed grand jury investigation.

Apple wasn't quite sweating but I could see his confidence wasn't there. I'm sure if he could have dumped it all at mine or Rick's feet he would have without hesitation.

Of course, I was rooting for a quick end that would put the whole smelly, rotten bunch on a garbage barge to St. Somewhere.

Chapter 22

All the calculations added up to me having two sexual predators on the payroll, a principal who should be on an 18th century Pirate ship, a superintendent apparently headed for the Superintendents' Hall of Fame and a school board so corrupt they make the Saudi Civil Service look upscale. Oh yeah, and myself under investigation by a District Attorney with ambition.

I started to wonder how it is I wound up at Sunnydale. Obviously, I'd made some incredibly bad choices to have wound up connected to this bunch. But what were they? Everything I did seemed logical to me. I broke no laws; I had acted in good faith, paid my bills on time, worked my way through college, taught during the day and went to class nights to get my administrator's certificate. What gives?

After I explained the whole theater situation to her, Dairy said she understood. And I believe she did intellectually, even if she couldn't accept the situation emotionally. She accepted what I had done as right but it just didn't feel right.

After about a thousand apologies by me she was willing to move on, but I sensed she was coming to the end of her rope as far as Sunnydale was concerned. One more incident like the movie theater and she'd probably be out there telling all her friends that even though it was the best sex she'd ever had, I wasn't worth it.

The amazing thing about this, I concluded after much contemplation, is that the adults and the students all committed the same misbehaviors. You would think there would be a vast difference between the adults and the students, but there really wasn't.

All these thoughts were spinning in my head and I could see they were making me feel worse. I got up, grabbed my suit jacket and headed out of my office towards the second floor. I knew that a few minutes with the students would cheer me up.

I got up to the second floor and started to wander towards the Home Ec. Room. As I was passing, I saw Mr. Duck's class just putting their books away. I glanced at my watch and was happy to see that he was only shaving four minutes off the end of class as opposed to the usual ten minutes. Then I remembered Mr. White was subbing in there today.

Mr. White and I had sat down in my office and discussed the whole mish-mash his run-in with Ted Brown had become. I assured him that no one involved in the whole deal found him responsible and that he should forget about it. He wanted to know what would happen to the kid. That was a sticky area though.

Even after the NAACP cleared Mr. White, the mom still insisted that her son had been the victim of racism. Without parental support the punishment would have little effectiveness. Instead of changing the kid's behavior it would probably generate more misbehavior. There was also the fact that too much time had passed since the infraction.

Mr. White couldn't understand any of this. As one who spent his life playing by the rules and working in organizations that more closely followed their mission, a modern day public school was a little hard for him to take.

I looked at him and wondered if America was running out of people like him. Or perhaps the ratio of guys like him to guys like Lou Mustard and Dr. Mayonnaise was shifting against America's favor.

"How's the Jaguar?" I asked after we'd finished discussing the Ted Brown case.

"Oh fine, I was playing it last night."

"You know I saw one of them go for nearly thirty thousand dollars the other day on one of those internet sales sites."

"Thirty thousand, wowww," he said slowly. "I didn't even know that they went for that much. I paid four hundred dollars for it and I had to borrow that from my father."

"Do you have it insured?"

"No, I never thought about it before."

"I think you should get it appraised to get a handle on what they really go for. I don't know if that website is a reliable source. Could be a bunch of wackos for all I know."

"Yeah."

"Then go to your insurance guy and get it covered."

"Yeah, you're right, I should do that."

"I'm probably going to steal it from you in the near future. You might as well get something for your troubles."

He started laughing about a beat too late, which told me I'd caught him off guard.

He got up and went to the door and said, "Don't steal it till after I get the policy on it. Okay?"

As I approached Mr. Duck's classroom I could see Mr. White was sitting at the teacher's desk watching the students prepare to leave. I stepped into the room and placed my palms out and said, "Children of Earth, be not afraid, I only wish to observe you and learn more of this thing you call Science class!"

At least three of four voices yelled out, "Hey Mr. Farmer!"

A chubby kid in the first row said with a smile, "Mr. Farmer you always be funnin'." The other students shot him looks of derision. They are in tenth grade and it is no longer cool to laugh at anything the adults say. I knew their resistance was high, but with a few well-placed jokes I could win them over.

I waited a second for everyone to finish putting their books into the evacuation positions. When the bell rang, they would all get up and get out of class in a hurry to be late for their next class. School is a subtle form of torture to most students.

"How is everyone today?"

The responses ranged from a nod of the head to a courtly "Wazzup?"

"Glad to hear it."

One student gave me an opening line as if on cue, "Mr. Farmer, you married?" I never wear my wedding ring. I can't say why exactly, but maybe it had something to do with my nearly losing it when we were first married and Dairy threatened that if I lost it, the next one was going through my nose.

"Married, are you crazy?" I said, as if he'd asked me to invest in horseshoe futures. "I knew a guy who got married once. . . and he died. . . True story!"

"Aw, Mr. Farmer, you just be funnin' again."

"No, it's true, marriage changes a man. Mr. White here was married last year and he was twenty-two years old at the time. Now look at him!"

They all broke up at that. It was good to see them laugh and be happy, even if it was a brief moment.

"Mebbe you gay!" yelled a large kid seated in back who wasn't happy that the class was warming.

"Easy there Tupac-the-Boor, we were having a pleasant conversation."

The class laughed at the heckler and that shut him up. Nothing is more feared by a high schooler than public humiliation. You have to be careful how you go about it however, because if the kids think you are being abusive toward the heckler they will turn on you fast.

Mr. White got a kick out of being in on my marriage joke. He had been married over forty years. It was good for him to laugh. He adored the kids but had very few good moments with them.

"Do you all want to know why I never married?" I said with a serious air, as if the memory welling up in me was painful and my joking had stopped.

"Yeah," they all started saying, many sitting up in an unconscious telegraph of their interest.

"Once, when I was a young man, not much older than many of you," I said with all seriousness, "I sailed on a big ship and I met a beautiful girl who was traveling first class. She was supposed to marry a rich guy she didn't really love. She didn't want to but her mom was really pushing her to marry him." I paused and let my eyes meet with theirs. I could see they were totally sucked in by my tragic tale of woe.

"I was traveling third class but we hit it off and started to see each other for dinner and such. Then one night, just as we realized we were crazy in love despite all our differences, the ship hit an iceberg. It started to sink rapidly."

I paused and it clicked with about half the class. They started exploding in laughter. The other half of the class started to look around confused. I continued on.

"We found ourselves on a raft that could only support one of us, so I pushed her off and floated over to a rescue boat. I never saw her again. And that is why I never married-- crashed love."

Now all the students were laughing, the heckler included. No doubt several students didn't get the joke but they were swept up in the laughter of their peers. The herd mentality kicked in and they were as much its victims as my doomed love boat was of that recalcitrant iceberg.

"Mr. Farmer you whack!" one girl said through her tears.

"I don't know of this 'whack' you speak of, but I'll take that remark as a compliment."

I walked to the door and raised my arms like I was going to give a sermon on the mount.

They all quieted instantly. I said, "A little learning is a dangerous thing. Drink deep, or taste not the Pierian Spring," and right on cue the bell rang and I stepped out of the classroom.

I headed down to the office to check some paperwork but I was feeling better. My time with the students although brief turned out to be the best part of my day. When I got back to my office Mr. Rabbit was there waiting for me.

Mr. Rabbit was a relative newcomer to Sunnydale. He'd been hired to take over for a certain Math teacher who'd recently departed. He was a slight man who despite only being in his late twenties was nearly bald. He had sharp features and a great sense of humor. I knew it was bad when I saw him waiting to speak with me.

"Ay, Mr. Rabbit, you wanted to see me?"

"Yeah, I can't do this," he blurted out like he had been holding his breath while waiting for me.

"Math?" I queried, trying to buy a little time for me to think and him to cool his jets.

"No, I mean be a teacher here. I can't do this."

I closed the door, sat down, then motioned for him to take a seat. He hesitated for a second, as if taking a seat would cause him to lose his resolve.

"You just started here."

"I know but I just can't do it."

"What exactly is the problem?"

"It's the kids I . . . I just can't take them. I don't think this is going to work out. I . . . I just can't do my best under these circumstances. I shouldn't be here if I can't do my best. These kids are so aggressive."

"Mr. Rabbit . . .Stanley, you just started here. You have to give it time. Our students are loud and seem scary but they're not bad. You just have to get used to them. If it were a perfect world, women's breasts would produce beer."

He laughed at the last remark and the pall of negativity he was under evaporated. I spent the next fifteen minutes convincing him to stay. He said he would but I could see he had already made his mind up. Three days later he submitted his resignation and four days later I was called to the superintendent's office to account for it.

Mr. Rabbit had different expectations of how students should behave. Teaching is a high stress job with little monetary reward. The truth is, a great many teachers quit before their fifth year. In the end, he secured a job in a college town up North near his only sister and an apartment near the co-ed dorms. I gotta admit, more than half of me wanted to go with him.

Chapter 23

On my way back from the cafeteria I ran into Apple in the main hallway. He said, "Take a walk with me."

We rarely discussed any business outside one of the principals' offices so I thought he needed me as a backup for some crisis that was brewing- you never knew at Sunnydale. I fell into step with him and we headed down the main hall towards the gym area.

As was my lifelong habit I said nothing until the boss spoke first. But Apple didn't say anything, which was a big deal because he usually kept up a constant stream of babble as if he had a bomb in his innards set to detonate should he ever stop talking.

He finally broke the silence just as we got to the heavy steel doors at the end of the hallway leading to the outside. He said, "This grand jury thing is almost over."

"Great!" I said.

I wasn't being disingenuous, although as one at the very bottom of the administrative ladder, who could blame me if I had been? I was happy for Rick. As the only honest administrator at Sunnydale besides myself, he took it hard. He knew he was swimming with sharks and he could handle himself, but it still hurt him to have his integrity questioned.

After my interview for Assistant Principal at Sunnydale, Rick was tasked with giving me a tour of the building. Although he was pleasant and helpful I could see that he was agitated. I assumed he was either annoyed at being asked to perform so mundane a task or he didn't like me. Later I found out that he held Sunnydale in such low regard he'd felt guilty about being part of talking me into working there. He actually apologized to me for it!

I told him that he had nothing to apologize for. The truth is, my sharp mind had picked up quite a bit of information about the place before my dull mind shut it up and accepted the position on its behalf. Rick had nothing to do with my stupidity.

Still, if the grand jury thing was coming to a close, what was with the cloak-and-dagger routine by Principal Fathead? We walked around to the back of the building to the point most remote from the axis of evil that was the district office before he said any more.

"Yeah, in order to get Lou for perjury they have to have two people who were willing to stand up and be witnesses. They only have one," he said.

"Wow. I wonder if there is anyone else who could be a witness?"

"There is someone and I know who it is."

I could see he was beaming. He was bursting to tell me something.

"Who?" I asked directly, thinking we were both a little old to be playing 'I know something you don't know!'

"Eddie Angle."

"Oh man, you can't turn him over to those guys! The man is a forty-five year old child."

I wasn't real fond of Eddie since I had a run-in with him the second month of school. He had wanted to go on a field trip with one of the classes and asked me for permission to go. I wasn't averse to him going on a trip, but the idiot asked me literally two minutes before the busses were set to leave.

When I told him that he couldn't go because I had nobody to sub for him he got very irate. He started yelling and cursing at me right there in the hallway. I ushered him away from the kids and down to my office.

Apple had heard the commotion of Eddie and I coming into the main office because Eddie was calling me a "Fucking asshole," as loud as he could.

We all wound up in my office and Apple and I let Eddie yell himself out. Once he'd calmed down a bit, we discussed the matter. Apple and I took turns trying to explain to Eddie why his behavior was unacceptable and that we have protocols for going on field trips, etc. It took us some time to get him to see he wasn't being abused by anyone.

Eddie started to say that he had been having emotional problems in his personal life because a woman he'd been dating for two years decided to go back to her husband. It seems, according to Eddie, that Eddie was a well endowed, talented lover who was just going with this woman for kicks, but then it turned serious.

Eddie started to cry and then plunged into the second half of the story. The woman he'd been pleasuring with his unique talents initially left her fabulously wealthy husband because the husband refused to leave the attic of their home and had been up there for two years.

At this point in the story I was biting down on my inner cheek to keep from exploding in laughter. Eddie however, started crying even harder. He had his elbows on his knees with his head in his hands and he was looking down as he talked.

The rich guy in the attic somehow convinced his ex-wife, Eddie's paramour, to give their lofty love another try. She broke down and, despite the great sex Eddie was doling out, decided to break Eddie's heart.

Eddie concluded his story by saying that screaming and cursing at me was really a function of his unrequited love and that he was sorry and I shouldn't think we weren't pals.

I never thought we were pals and this whole episode took me to a place I didn't want to go, but I hadn't the heart to convey any of my thoughts to him. I thought I had done enough by not laughing hysterically at the part about the rich guy not being able to leave the attic.

Eddie had stopped crying and started to wipe away the tears and his runny nose then said, "Hey, Mr. Farmer I'm sorry about calling you a fucking asshole," extending his hand out to shake mine.

I instinctively reached out and shook his hand. It was wet with his tears and mucous and I was horrified the instant I touched it. I actually wished I was back on the flypaper floor of the movie theater. It was awful.

I unconsciously placed my other hand around my wrist as if it was a tourniquet preventing the germs I knew were all over my hand from traveling to the rest of my body. I stood up and said, "No problem Mr. Angle, I understand. Excuse me, I'll be right back."

As soon as I got out the door of my office I shot down to the men's room and washed both my hands for ten minutes.

Now, Apple was telling me that Angle knew something the DA could use to bag Lou. I wasn't too sure about this because I couldn't see Angle knowing anything of importance, and what kind of credibility could a guy like him have anyway? But I also knew that if it were true and it did come to pass that Angle was instrumental in getting Lou kicked off the board and/or put in jail, then Angle could forget ever working at Sunnydale again and his connection to the sports program he lived for would be severed forever.

I had little reason to champion anything that could even remotely be considered Angle's cause. But there had been enough victims of Lou Mustard's and Dr. Mayonnaise's malfeasance already. That's why I had said to Apple, "Oh man, you can't turn him over to those guys! The man is a forty-five year old child."

"The Superintendent told me not to talk with anyone so I'm not gonna say anything. I always do what I'm told," Apple said.

Chapter 24

I couldn't imagine why Apple had told me about the Eddie Angle thing. I had no role in all this. It was bad enough I made the comment about Eddie before checking Apple for a wire. The whole conversation was perplexing.

The following day I checked my mail just before going out to watch the kids leave. In addition to some junk mail concerning textbooks and promotional tee shirts, there was a first draft of the DA's report on the grand jury investigation, put there by an anonymous hand.

The question of who put the rough draft of a super-secret document in my mailbox was like the Kennedy assassination. You had to ask, who had the motive, who had access, what the point of the act was, and most importantly, who the fuck did it?

I didn't have a great deal of time to play this game of whodunit and the truth is, there were a number of players who could have done it. And after I read it, something I did right away despite having the knowledge that it was probably illegal to do so, the mystery became more mysterious and therefore nearly impossible to solve.

The report basically said that while there was a great deal of incompetence in the leadership at Sunnydale, there was insufficient proof to bring charges against anyone. The report also went on to criticize many of the practices at Sunnydale.

The report had many factual errors, not the least of which was a charge that our Alternative Education program was in violation of the law when the program had been approved by the state's Department of Education just before I was hired. It also seemed to sensationalize trivial matters that are endemic to all schools. It made no mention of the fact, in the part concerning Ms.

Siren, that their detective told us she was not doing anything inappropriate.

In short, the report was full of spin and questionable grammar. The stupid bastards split infinitives and dangled participles all over the place. I would have given the DA a "C" for it.

The content of the report made answering the question of who left it in my box harder to answer because I could see that there was sufficient motivation on both sides. Lou and Mayonnaise maybe wanted me to know that they were going to be let off so it would do me no good to offer any assistance to the other side, not that I ever gave any cause for them to think I would. The DA and or the police department maybe sent it to me hoping the news that these guys were going to get off would spur me to act in some way that would help them.

Apple maybe wanted me to know just to spur me to do something stupid enough to get myself fired. Even Rick might have put it there, but I couldn't think of a reason he would nor could I believe he would ever do something so seedy. I even speculated that maybe it was a case of a drunken athletic director putting it in the wrong box.

No matter who was responsible for supplying me with the report, the ultimate desire was to manipulate me in some way. I just couldn't figure out which way, but I supposed in the end it didn't matter. Whatever I chose to do I would have to do it for my own reasons. After all, if there was one thing that was clear to me, it was that as a school administrator, I was on my own. I was definitely walking the wire without a net.

The report didn't say anywhere on it when it was going to be published. I had no idea how much time I had before it was a done deal. In the world of decisions, having to make one fast about a complex situation of which little is known is the worst possible scenario. I learned never to make a decision any faster than I have to and here I was faced with not knowing how long I had to decide about this confusion.

I decided to act. I turned the matter over to my sharp mind. I can't explain what motivated me exactly. I can say that it wasn't for Eddie. He was, to my mind, a minor concern. I would love to say that I did it for the kids, but that would only be partially true. They had already been abused and no act by me could undo that. I sure as hell wasn't out for justice because I knew better than anyone that only exists in heaven.

Thucydides once remarked, "The strong do what they can and the weak suffer what they must." I guess I had decided to act because mostly I was pissed that the strong were about to get away with doing what they can while the weak suffered. Lou and Mayonnaise were about to get away with it all and I didn't want that to happen. I didn't want them to go on with their systematic theft of the quality education due the powerless students of Sunnydale.

My sharp mind had come up with a plan that was both brilliant and stupid at the same time. I was well aware that such a plan was exactly the sort required to get anything done at Sunnydale.

I called Lou and told him that I needed to see him before he went to the school board meeting. I told him it was important and that I wanted to discuss it in my office. It was an unusual request, but I knew he'd pull himself out of Biffy's mother's bed a few minutes early under the paranoid assumption that he couldn't afford to not know what cards I was holding.

I was at my desk going over the plan one more time in my head when I heard the front office door open. He was right on time. I could hear him huffing as he worked his bulk from the front entrance to the door of my office.

"Hey Lou, thanks for coming down."

"Let's make this fast. Da school board meeting be startin soon and I gotta be there."

"Okay Lou, I wanted to discuss your resignation with you," I said, going straight to it. I wanted him off balance with no time to calculate.

"That's not going to happen," he said quickly.

"Actually, I think it is."

"Why should I resign? You be the one having everyone arrested around here and acting all better than everybody!"

"Lou, I know you were instrumental in getting Stubby a job here. I also know you've been monkeying with the Grand Jury investigation."

"What have I been doing with the Grand Jury?"

"You've been discussing the case with a jury member. That's called jury tampering, perhaps obstruction of justice as well."

"You have no proof a dat!"

"Lou, I also know what you did with Stubby."

"What'd I do with Stubby?"

"You overlooked his criminal past so he could work here. You and Dr. Mayonnaise knew all about it."

He didn't say anything to that. He just stared at me. Probably thought I was wearing a wire. I could see he was hunkered down and perfectly willing to wait out the storm. That was not good for me. I had to get him out of his hole.

I started by saying, "I know you thought you were doing a favor for a kid you coached in Pee Wee football. I know you thought you were doing the right thing, but Lou, you let a fox in the henhouse and a lot of good kids paid the price for that mistake."

"You don't have no proof I knew anything."

"Oh, I have a great deal of proof insofar as Stubby is concerned."

I reached behind my desk and pulled up a fairly stuffed, accordion file folder. I held it up and said, "It seems your nephew isn't the only person who got a hold of a key he shouldn't have. It also seems Mr. Superintendent kept very precise records of everything he did and every conversation he had."

"You can't turn over stolen records to the District Attorney. He be arresting *you*," he said, as if he were saying check mate.

"Well, I have no intention of falling on my sword. I don't have to give him anything. They'll be sent by courier addressed to your friend the District Attorney from an anonymous, but concerned, citizen."

He stopped to consider all this. I could see the wheels were turning. He shifted in his seat and looked away in thought.

"Look, Lou, I am not so much concerned about justice in the universe as I am the students of this school. You could do them and yourself a favor by resigning. You resign and I lose this packet and the copies in my Lawyer's office will remain there for good. If I hand this over, the DA is going to be on you like polyester on a fat ass and I know you know what that's like."

"You really think you so smart. You ain't so smart you know!" he said, boiling.

"Well, maybe not. Nevertheless, I have taken the liberty of writing your resignation letter for you. I kept it simple but I want you to read it and sign it now."

This was the critical moment. I had spent my whole life being a loyal supporter of the regime and now I was stepping out into rebellion. There was no turning back and my renegade act had a cold feeling, scary but exciting. It also gave me a sensation of power that served as its own justification. Heady stuff indeed.

I placed the documents folder on the edge of my desk, out of his reach but clearly in sight, and placed the prepared document in front of him. I put a pen next to it. He sighed heavily after reading it and glared at me. I didn't twitch a muscle even though my internal organs were banging around my insides like bees in a jar. He grabbed the pen and signed it as if he were ripping off a band aid.

In Afghanistan they would describe my predicament as trying to stand on two watermelons. You probably figured out that I was bluffing. I had nothing. Force equals mass times acceleration plus bullshit.

Chapter 25

One week after Lou announced his decision to resign from the board, Doctor Mayonnaise announced his decision to retire due to health reasons. I didn't have to strong-arm him. I simply mentioned my opinion that with Lou out of the picture he was the last man standing as far as the DA's attention was concerned. He was mad as hell but he saw the logic of it. That was a risky move too, but since the DA hadn't yet produced his toothless grand jury report, I figured it would work.

One week after the Sith Lord of the District Office announced his early retirement, I cleared out my office and said my good-byes. I am terrible with good-byes. But then, many weren't too sad to see me go. Not because they disliked me personally, but because the constant turnover of administrators worked to keep anyone from keeping track of them. There were quite a few employees who felt their long term success was enhanced by the chaos. I was the third Assistant Principal to hold my position at Sunnydale in three years.

My health hadn't fared well. I had a constant headache, I was having difficulty breathing at times and the fingers on my right hand took to twitching by themselves, so much so that sometimes I had to hold them with my left to keep people from noticing. In any case, it was time to get out of Dodge.

I didn't hold anything against the people at Sunnydale however. It is hard to hate people who are so self-destructive. I even told Biffy that she'd done a good job as my secretary. I don't think she believed me. I know I didn't. But she thanked me just the same.

I was exiting through the main entrance when I ran into Elvina Denton. This time I saw her coming. She was walking up to the front doors using a cane. My time at Sunnydale had made us both older. Still, she walked with a dignified defiance of time.

"Howdy Mr. Farmer, How y'all doin taday?"

"I've never been better," I said, lying easily as if I were a veteran superintendent. "How about you?"

"Fine, jes fine."

I was glad she was fine and I lied to her because there was no reason to burden her with my problems. But I knew just as surely as she was in the last years of her life, I was in the last few minutes of my career as an administrator. With Sunnydale as my former employer and no references, I had virtually no chance I'd ever run a school again.

Usually, my thoughts of Sunnydale stampede through my mind and I have little defense against them. Lately, one has been consistently showing up just before I fall asleep. Especially on days I try in vain to get another administration job.

It was my second to last day at Sunnydale. Mr. White brought his Fender Jaguar by the school when he was taking it to be appraised. We took a walk out to the parking lot where he had it stashed in the back of his car. I got to play it for a little while.

In a way that guitar reminded me of Sunnydale. It occurred to me in the brief time I held it in my arms that it was a shame such a fine instrument should be in the hands of such a poor musician. As I put it away, just before I closed the case, when I was sure no one could hear me, I whispered, "I love you."

www.ingramcontent.com/pod-product-compliance
Lightning Source LLC
Chambersburg PA
CBHW071328190426
43193CB00041B/933